# Forgiveness

# ADAM HAMILTON

# Forgiveness

Finding Peace Through Letting Go

ABINGDON PRESS
NASHVILLE

FORGIVENESS
FINDING PEACE THROUGH LETTING GO

*Copyright © 2012 by Adam Hamilton*
*All rights reserved.*

This book is printed on elemental chlorine–free paper.
ISBN 978-1-5018-5849-9

**The Library of Congress has cataloged the hardcover edition as follows:**

https://lccn.loc.gov/2012022583
Hamilton, Adam, 1964- Forgiveness : finding peace through letting go / Adam Hamilton. Nashville, TN : Abingdon Press, c2012.

142 p. ; 19 cm.
BV4647.F55 H355 2012
ISBN: 9781426742644 (hbk. : alk. paper) 9781426740442 (hbk. : alk. paper)

18 19 20 21 22 23 24 25 26 27 — 10 9 8 7 6 5 4 3 2 1
MANUFACTURED IN THE UNITED STATES OF AMERICA

To Dan Entwistle, Managing Executive Director at the Church of the Resurrection, on this twentieth year of ministry at the church. Dan's grace-filled ministry has had a profound impact upon so many lives, including my own.

# CONTENTS

# SIX WORDS

Forgiveness is essential to our lives. Without it, no marriage can survive, no family can stay together, and no society can be sustained. It is a necessary part of lasting friendships and work relationships.

The reason lies in an inescapable fact of human nature: we are bound to hurt others, and others are bound to hurt us. If we are to live successfully, and if we are ever to know freedom and joy, these six words must be a regular part of our vocabulary: "I am sorry" and "I forgive you." If we lack the ability to say, "I am sorry," life will be immeasurably more difficult than it needs to be. If we can't bring ourselves to say, "I forgive you," life will be filled with bitterness and pain.

This book is not meant to be an exhaustive study on the topic of forgiveness. There are many excellent but much lengthier and more comprehensive books on the topic. Instead, this little book examines four common relationships in which we find ourselves in need of receiving or extending forgiveness: our relationship with God, with our spouses or romantic interests, with our parents and siblings, and with all others in our lives.

There are many dimensions to forgiveness, and each situation in which forgiveness is required is unique; there are circumstances that have led me to counsel individuals in ways different from what I describe in this book. But here, we will cover the big concepts surrounding forgiveness, as well as the most common relationships in which we find ourselves needing to give or receive it.

My hope is that all who read this book might find help and encouragement as they seek reconciliation and healing through the act of asking for, and extending, forgiveness.

# CHAPTER ONE

# THE DIVINE ANSWER

*Happy are those whose transgression is forgiven,*
*    whose sin is covered.*
*Happy are those to whom the LORD imputes no iniquity,*
*    and in whose spirit there is no deceit.*
*While I kept silence, my body wasted away*
*    through my groaning all day long.*
*For day and night your hand was heavy upon me;*
*    my strength was dried up as by the heat of summer.*
*Then I acknowledged my sin to you,*
*    and I did not hide my iniquity;*
*I said, "I will confess my transgressions to the LORD,"*
*    and you forgave the guilt of my sin.*
*            Psalm 32:1-5*

To all of the customers of the local florist who got sneezing powder in their flowers last Tuesday, I apologize. You were really not the intended victims. I just wanted to make you angry at the florist, my stingy employer. I wasn't trying to hurt you. Bill


I'm sorry. You were waiting for the car to get out of the parking place so you could back in. I slid in frontward—I *had* to do this because I was *desperate* to get into the store so I could use the men's room, and there were *no other spaces.* My apologies. I hope you read this and understand. Driver of gray Honda.


To all my high school classmates, I am so sorry for those mornings when I came to school without brushing my teeth. I don't know where I got the idea that if I didn't eat, I didn't need to brush. I know you tried to hint, but I didn't "get it."


For all the things that happened to you as a kid that I never knew about. Maybe you were told not to tell me, but I should have been there for you, and you should have been able to tell me anything. For the fact that you weren't and I wasn't, I am truly sorry. Mom

Recently, I discovered several websites on which people can anonymously post apologies like those above. Some who post on these sites apparently don't know how to reach those they have wronged. In the case of others, the person wronged is deceased. Still others seem unwilling or not yet prepared to apologize directly to the individuals. Some of the postings are humorous; some are far more weighty. I think all of us can find a part of ourselves in one of them.

In a sermon called "To Whom Much is Forgiven," twentieth-century existentialist theologian Paul Tillich offers a perspective that speaks to people such as the above, and to all of us. Tillich wrote, "Forgiveness is an answer, the divine answer, to the question implied in our existence" (*The New Being* [New York: Scribner's, 1955]).

I would suggest that there are at least three questions "implied in our existence," to which forgiveness is God's answer. For example, in the apology of the mother, if you are the child who has been wounded, who perhaps experienced abuse when you were little, and whose mother did nothing to stop it, the question implied is *How do I keep bitterness, anger, hate, or the desire for revenge from consuming me?* If you are the mother who feels great guilt because you didn't step in to stop the abuse, there are perhaps two questions implied: *How can I be reconciled to the one I wronged?* and *How can my burden of guilt be removed?*

Every one of us asks questions like these, and God's answer to each of them is forgiveness. While abuse may not have been a part of our story, at some point we've been wronged, at some point we've failed to intervene to stop someone else from being wronged, and in one way or another we've all wronged others. If we are not to spend our lives stumbling in the dark as wounded, angry human beings, we must know and carry with us the answer—God's answer: forgiveness.

## MAKING SENSE OF SIN

Making sense of forgiveness means talking about *sin,* a word certain to make some people cringe. It brings to mind preachers who use the word to beat people down, or to frighten and intimidate children, applying it to all sorts of acts that aren't really sin, from going to the movies to learning to dance. But understood correctly, the concept of sin is one that serves a very useful purpose in any discussion of forgiveness.

The Greek and Hebrew words most often translated as *sin* in the Bible refer to "missing the mark" (think archery and an arrow that misses the target) or "straying from the path" (picture someone wandering off a trail and getting hopelessly lost). The implication is that there is a mark, an ideal, or a path that we are meant to follow in order to have a proper relationship with others and with God. We are meant to love. We are meant to do justice. We are meant to care for people and put their needs before our own. We are meant to tell the truth, to be faithful, to do the kind and loving thing. If we did these things all the time, there would be no need for forgiveness.

I suspect that all of us, whether we have any religious

faith or not, could agree that there is a way we're meant to live, an ideal path we should take. We know, too, that most of us struggle in walking that path. We stray at times. In fact, it seems to be the human condition that we stray too often and too easily. We use the word *temptation* to describe those things that draw us away.

The Bible opens with a story of temptation, one that is the archetype or pattern for how we human beings have struggled and succumbed ever since. In the story of Adam and Eve in the Garden of Eden, God offered paradise if this first couple would obey a simple rule: don't eat from one tree. They could eat anything else they wanted, but, essentially, God said to them, "This one tree will bring harm to you and your offspring. This is the path: enjoy everything, and be fruitful and multiply. Just avoid that tree right over there." But, of course, that was the one tree they came most desperately to desire.

Some readers take the story literally, some figuratively, but nearly all agree that it points to our struggle with rules, with limits, and with the path. The story also points to the truth that, from the beginning, God gave humanity a profound, wonderful, and dreadful gift— freedom to walk in the path, or stray from it.

Sometimes, our straying from the path is inadvertent. I think of the last time I was pulled over for speeding. (Yes, it has happened more than once.) I truly did not mean to be going so fast. I told the officer as I handed him my license, "I'm sorry. I wasn't paying attention." That actually did not help my cause. Rather, he suggested that my comment was worthy of a second ticket!

On other occasions, we know the path but make a conscious decision to stray from it. We realize the path calls us to be honest, but being honest might lose us the deal, or cost us more taxes, or embarrass us. So, we step off the path, hoping no one finds out and planning to get back on somewhere down the way.

Yes, Adam and Eve's story is our story. Healthy autonomy turns to unhealthy ego. *I* become the most important thing in my life, the thing around which the entire universe revolves. I live my life with blinders on, thinking only, "How can I be happy? How can I be safe?" I begin to care less and less about you as I go after what benefits me. I ignore your feelings while seeking to avoid suffering myself. I fail to do the right and loving thing, and sometimes do the hurtful thing in my relationships with others. The more that happens, the further I get from the path. And when I hurt you, you may well hurt me, meaning we both move further from the ideal, and the gap between us widens. The distance between where we are and where we are meant to be, along with the things we have done to create that distance and the hurt it has caused for others, is all part of what we call sin. We feel sin as a wall around us, or a gulf between us and others. When we decide at last to close that gap, to heal the breach, we must seek out the answer God has provided: forgiveness.

But what is it we are actually looking for when we seek forgiveness? We are not asking the other person to excuse what we've done, but rather to pardon us. We are looking for reconciliation, for the restoration of our relationship. We are asking for that person to release the right to retaliate. When my wife LaVon and I have conflict, often the result of something insensitive I have said or done, my request for forgiveness is a plea that she not hold my sin between us, separating us from each other, but that she break down the wall, so I might be in right relationship with her again.

In seeking and finding forgiveness, we experience pardon and restoration, which offer a new beginning, and we return to the path.

## THE BURDEN OF GUILT AND SEPARATION FROM GOD

There is another party who is affected by any sin that we commit against another. When our action or inaction hurts someone, we're also wounding our relationship with God, for it is God's path we stray from. It may take time, but at some point, that additional breach begins to make itself known. As our sins pile up and the gap increases between the ideal and the actual, we begin to feel further and further removed from God. We pray, but our prayers don't seem to go anywhere. We no longer feel God's presence. After a while, we may wonder if God even exists. We struggle. Life becomes harder and harder, because we're not on the path God intended human beings to walk. The psalmist reflected the spiritual impact of our straying from God's path in the seven so-called Penitential Psalms. You can feel the angst the psalmist felt at being separated from God, and you can feel the weight of that sin. It is a weight we call guilt. In Psalm 32, part of which opens this chapter, the psalmist describes the feeling of alienation from God:

> For day and night your hand
>     was heavy upon me;
> my strength was dried up as
>     by the heat of summer.

Psalm 38, another of the Penitential Psalms, says, "My guilt has overwhelmed me / like a burden too heavy to bear" (NIV).

The idea of guilt being a burden is a powerful metaphor, and one I find very helpful. When we don't ask God's forgiveness, when we don't seek to be reconciled through repentance, we carry the guilt—the weight—of each and every sin with us. We may not even recognize it at first, since some of our sins seem fairly small to us. It was the way we made just a little insult or a tiny jab as we walked away from someone. It was how we treated the person at the cash register or the way we snapped at our spouse. Sometimes sins are more serious. They're the intentionally hurtful things we say and do over and over again. We carry around these sins, big and small, and as long as we don't confess and repent of them, they remain in our souls.

I sought to illustrate this idea to my congregation the last time I preached on forgiveness. I had a table on the chancel, covered in rocks of all shapes and sizes. Some rocks were small, just pebbles; others could be weighed in pounds. I had a backpack that represented the way we carry our sin and guilt with us. I took two handfuls of pebbles and named them things like Harsh Words, An Irritating Glance, Speeding, Little White Lies. When you tossed them into the backpack, you hardly felt it. But after adding handfuls of pebbles over time, the backpack became quite heavy.

The medium-sized rocks represented transgressions that were a bit more serious: the hurtful thing said to a spouse, the lie that was not so little, dishonest gain. I took those rocks and added them to the backpack. Such sins, left unaddressed, especially when repeated and eventually discovered, can bring serious pain to others. But even when they are not discovered, carrying enough of them on your back will weigh you down.

Then there were the big rocks, each stone the size of a bread loaf, some as heavy as twenty pounds. They represented very serious sins—the kind that, at work, for example, would merit our dismissal if discovered. Some might be criminal acts. Some represented such fundamental violations of trust that, if found out, would lead to divorce or a loss of friendships. I put a few of those in my backpack.

I took my backpack, now filled with nearly sixty pounds of rocks, hoisted it onto my back, and continued to preach and move around the chancel of the church. But quickly, I began to become winded. My shoulders drooped. One of my arms tingled, and my lower back hurt. The congregation winced as they watched, seeing the metaphorical effects of sin and guilt on our souls played out on my body as I sought to carry that pack while preaching. Like the psalmist, I could feel it: "My guilt has overwhelmed me, like a burden too heavy for me to carry."

Those who don't seek forgiveness carry a host of burdens. Every harsh word, every unclean thought, every instance in which we neglect to do the right thing or go ahead and do the wrong thing—they're all there. Without forgiveness, they create an ever-widening gap between us and God, and between us and our fellow human beings. They sap our joy and then our strength.

Fortunately, there is an answer. God's answer to "the question[s] implied in our existence" is that we seek God's forgiveness and the forgiveness of those we've wronged. Seeking forgiveness can lighten our load. It can set us free. It can restore us to a right relationship with God and others. For, as the psalmist attests, "God is rich in mercy and abounding in steadfast love."

Throughout the Scriptures, God says, in effect, "Let me lift the burden from you." In the Old Testament or Hebrew Bible, we find that God provided a whole system by which people could atone for their sins, because God wanted them to be healed and to live in right relationship with him. This theme of forgiveness and atonement is also a central focus of the New Testament. It is the good news of the gospel of Jesus Christ: God provided a Savior and offers us forgiveness and a new beginning.

## THE GOSPEL OF FORGIVENESS

More than any other world religion, Christianity teaches, preaches, veritably shouts forgiveness. Yes, some of our preachers dwell too long on guilt, and consequently many see Christianity as primarily a religion of guilt. That is unfortunate, for a Christianity obsessed with guilt is no Christianity. Christianity is a faith whose central focus is not guilt, but grace, redemption, healing, forgiveness, and mercy.

But the process of forgiveness begins with our awareness and understanding of sin, for if we are not aware of our sin, we go on living self-absorbed lives while hurting others. So the purpose of preaching and learning about sin is to open the door to healing!

Doctors study medicine not so they can go around telling people they are sick, but so they can *heal* those who are sick, and the healing can't start until patients are willing to admit they are sick. Once patients admit this, there is the important task of the diagnosis, which then makes possible the cure. So it is with Christianity. We speak about sin in an attempt to diagnose the spiritual malady that afflicts us all. My goal, then, is not to accuse you of being, or even to tell you that, you are sick, but to offer you the medicine that makes you well. It's not simply to ask you the question, but to lead you to the answer. Yes, we're all sinners, and yes, this is a serious issue, but God is a God of grace and mercy.

The psalmist says it this way in Psalm 103:8-12:

> The LORD is merciful and gracious,
> > slow to anger and abounding in steadfast love . . .
> He does not deal with us according to our sins,
> > nor repay us according to our iniquities.
> For as the heavens are high above the earth,
> > so great is his steadfast love toward those who
> > fear him;
> as far as the east is from the west,
> > so far he removes our transgressions from us.

God wants to relieve us of the burden that comes with a life of sin, and to set our feet back on the right path. That is precisely why Jesus came. His life and ministry are defined by forgiveness. It was a mission laid out for him before he was born. He was still in the womb when the angel spoke to Joseph and said, "Fear not to take Mary as your wife, for that which is conceived of her is of the Holy Spirit. And when this child is born you shall call him Jesus, which means savior, for he will save his people from their sins" (Matthew 1:20-21).

Story after story in the gospels involves Jesus' ministry with "sinners." He constantly reached out to those who were estranged from God. He was even accused by the pious of his day of eating with sinners. The stories he told, like the beautiful parable of the Prodigal Son, point to God's gracious love and grace toward all of us who have made foolish decisions and turned from God's path.

Once, while Jesus was teaching, the religious leaders brought to him a woman caught in the act of adultery.

The leaders were carrying stones, since the penalty for adultery, according to the Law of Moses, was death by stoning. They brought the woman to Jesus, hoping to trap him because they knew he showed grace to sinners. They asked him, "Jesus, what shall we do with this woman?" To which he replied, "The one of you who is without sin, you cast the first stone." One by one, the religious leaders walked away. Then Jesus turned to the woman. She was ashamed and filled with guilt, but he looked at her and said, "Woman, where are your accusers? Neither do I condemn you. Go and sin no more" (John 8:10-11).

Beyond the parables he taught and the ministry he wrought with sinners, we have Jesus' direct teaching on our need to receive and offer forgiveness, which we hear in the prayer he taught us to pray: "Forgive us our trespasses (or debts)," it says, "as we forgive those who trespass against us."

Jesus did as he taught. He forgave the tax collectors, prostitutes, and adulterers. At the Last Supper, he took wine and said to his disciples, "Drink this cup, for it is my blood of the new covenant poured out for you and for many for the forgiveness of sins." In this, he offered himself as an amends—an atoning sacrifice—for the sins of the world. Later, as he hung on the cross, he demonstrated the ultimate in forgiveness, praying for those who were putting him to death. "Father," he said, "forgive them, for they know not what they do."

Finally, shortly after his resurrection, Jesus commanded his disciples to announce the forgiveness of sins. "Whomever you forgive," he told them, "I forgive."

Let's return to Psalm 103 and read through this passage again.

> The LORD is merciful and gracious,
>     slow to anger and abounding in steadfast love . . .
> He does not deal with us according to our sins,
>     nor repay us according to our iniquities.
> For as the heavens are high above the earth,
>     so great is his steadfast love toward those who
>     fear him;

as far as the east is from the west,
  so far he removes our transgressions from us.

This is the extravagant grace that is God's heart and character. It is something we know in our heads, and yet we often struggle to accept it in our hearts. We sometimes fail to understand and experience God's grace, which is offered freely to us, continuing to carry burdens of separation or guilt that God has already sought to remove.

I asked people in our congregation about their struggles with forgiveness and got plenty of responses. One of them really captured what many said they felt: "I struggle almost daily. I can see how God works in others' lives, but in my own, I struggle. I know that God loves me no matter what I've done or been in my life, but to really feel it at the core of my being, I struggle."

Another said, "In the military, I took lives. I spent years filled with guilt because of this. Having been in close combat situations where you are looking at a person while taking their life changes you. It was impossible to imagine God forgiving me for something that I could not forgive myself for doing."

Some time ago, I saw a man outside of church and said, "I haven't seen you for a while. Where have you been?"

"I am having a hard time coming back to church," he said. "I did something I'm really ashamed of, and I just...I just feel like I can't come back."

"Don't you understand?" I said. "That's where you need to be. The church is for sinners!"

Then there was a conversation I had not long ago with a woman in her fifties who said to me, "I've never told anybody this before, but when I was in my twenties I got pregnant. I was scared and decided to have an abortion. But after the abortion, I calculated the date the child would have been born, and every year for the last thirty years during that month, I think about the child I might have had.

It was clear that this woman still carried a burden, even

thirty years later. It was not wrong for her to remember the baby she aborted, but even in that case, God longs for that woman to know his grace and forgiveness. Each of us has done things we regret and cannot change. We cringe or even cry when we think of them. And yet often we carry these burdens unnecessarily. We fail to trust that God is gracious and merciful, slow to anger and abounding in steadfast love, and that "as far as the east is from the west, so far shall he remove our sins from us." Through it all, God's message to us remains the same: Stop carrying the burden yourself. Let me take it. Be reconciled to me.

This is the thing to remember: God has *already* agreed to that reconciliation. Tillich, in another of his sermons, said that the bottom line of faith is accepting God's acceptance of you. When you turn to God and long to be with him, he is already reaching out, waiting for you with open arms. God has done everything necessary for your forgiveness, and he offers that forgiveness freely. All you have to do to gain this grace—grace that came at such a terrific price—is to accept it.

## REPENTANCE

Availing myself of God's offer and finding relief from the weight of my sin is a matter of repentance. The Greek word for repentance is *metanoia,* a word that means to have a change of heart that results in a change of behavior. Depending upon the nature of the sin, repentance may include strong feelings of remorse, or it may simply be a conviction that the path one had taken was the wrong path, coupled with a determination to live differently in the future.

Repentance begins with my awareness of the gap I have created between myself and God, or myself and the other person. I acknowledge that I have stepped off the path, hurting people and wounding my relationship with God, and I express the remorse I feel. I confess to the other person and do what I can to make amends, I confess to God and ask for his mercy and forgiveness, and I turn back toward the right.

When I do that, God forgives me. It's not a complicated

process. God removes the burden of my sin and I am re-stored. The psalmist captures the process in Psalm 32:5:

> Then I acknowledged my sin to you,
>     and I did not hide my iniquity;
> I said, "I will confess my transgressions to the LORD,"
>     and you forgave the guilt of my sin.

This same process guides our efforts at reconciliation with others. There are times when I will do or say things that are hurtful to LaVon and find that we're in conflict with each other. When I come to understand the situation and my role in it, I begin to feel its weight. I sense the gap existing in our relationship. I think, "Why did I say that? It was really hurtful. It was stupid. God asked me to love this woman, and I do love her, but I didn't act lovingly toward her." So I come back to her and say, "LaVon, I really am sorry for what I said. I know it hurt you, and I don't want to do that again. I'm really sorry."

In response, she almost always does the same thing. She wraps her arms around me and says, "I love you."

When I feel that embrace from her, it gives me a picture, a glimpse, of what God does when we repent, and what it feels like to be reconciled to him.

On the Sunday I carried that backpack with its sixty pounds of rocks, I finally demonstrated what happens when we repent and God forgives, and we are reconciled to him. I dropped the backpack to the floor. Suddenly, without all that weight on my back, I felt that I could fly! That's what happens when you confess and then trust that God has forgiven you. You can breathe again. You can *dance* again. You can run and not grow weary, walk and not faint, because you've experienced the grace of God.

That's exactly what God wants for you.

It's important to recognize, however, that God will not be toyed with. Don't pretend you're seeking forgiveness if you're really not. The kind of half-hearted apologies we sometimes offer don't cut it here. True repentance is the heartfelt recognition that we've done wrong and strayed from the path. It's a genuine sense that we don't want to do or say that thing again, and a desire to walk on the right path once more. The process is finalized when we decide to stop heading in the wrong direction and come back to the right path.

One of the first stories I ever shared in a sermon on forgiveness came from Ron Lee Davis's book *A Forgiving God in an Unforgiving World*. I have always loved the story, and it is worth retelling here.

There was a much-loved priest in the Philippines who carried the burden of a secret sin he had committed many years earlier. Although he had led many to the mercy of Christ, he struggled with his own transgression. He had repented, but he couldn't accept that God had forgiven him. For decades afterward, he felt no peace.

A woman in his parish who loved God deeply claimed to have regular dreams and visions in which she spoke with Christ and he with her. People from all over the islands came to speak with her, bringing questions for her to take to the Lord and then waiting for the answers she brought back. The priest was skeptical, but he dared to hope just a little. He decided to put her to the test. One day he went to her and said, "When I was back in seminary, I did something wrong. No one else knows anything about it. The next time you talk to Jesus, I would like you to ask him what that sin was. If he tells you, I'll know you were really talking to him."

Although he presented it as a test, what the priest really hoped was that this woman might say something that would relieve the awful guilt he'd carried for all these years.

The hours turned to days and the days into nearly two weeks when finally the woman came to him again.

"Well," he said, "did you have any of your visions? Did you speak with Jesus?"

"Yes, I did," she said.

"Did you talk to him . . . about my question?" There was no hiding his agitation.

"Yes," she said, "I did."

"Did he answer you?"

"Yes, as a matter of fact, he did," she said.

By now his heart was pounding and beads of sweat were forming at his temples. "Well, what did he say?"

"I told him, 'My priest committed a sin when he was in seminary,'" she said. "'He is still burdened by it. He wants to know if you know what that sin was.' Jesus looked right at me and he said, 'Ah, yes. Your priest's sin. Funny thing, I just don't remember it anymore'" (Ron Lee Davis, *A Forgiving God in an Unforgiving World* [Eugene, Ore.: Harvest House, 1984]).

Jesus doesn't forget our sins. Rather, he chooses not to remember them. The "new covenant" Jesus referred to at the Last Supper is a reference to Jeremiah 31:31-34, where God says, "I will make a new covenant with my people Israel. I will write my law on their hearts. They will all know me from the least to the greatest. And I will forgive their iniquity. And I will remember their sin no more."

The choice is yours. You can continue to carry the

burden of your sins, or you can allow the Lord to take it from you and set you free, as he wants to do.

Some of you live in grace, not really struggling with past sins. You have given them to God and don't think about them. You may just need to say, "Lord, for the things I did this past week that took me from the path, and for the ways I failed to do what you wanted me to do, please forgive me." Then simply trust in his grace.

But others of you are carrying heavy burdens from the past. God knows them. Christ has already suffered for them. He stands there, longing to take you into his arms. He's saying to you, "Please let them go. Please give them to me."

The process begins with acknowledgment and sorrow. You might say simply, "Lord, I'm really sorry for what I did." Speak to him as though he were a concerned and loving parent, or a good friend you have wronged. Confess and ask him to forgive you and to take the burden from you. Then turn back toward the path, saying, "Lord, make me new. Give me strength to walk in the path that you have prepared for me."

Trust that Jesus has already borne your sins on the cross, and that "as far as the east is from the west, so far shall the LORD remove your sin from you." Know that you can come away from the encounter with joy in your heart and a spring in your step, loved, forgiven, and free.

After all, that is the good news of the Christian gospel.

## THINKING IT THROUGH

• If you were going to post an anonymous apology at one of the websites mentioned earlier, what would it be? Write out the apology, and then reflect on how the apology made you feel.

• What other questions can you think of that, as Paul Tillich expressed it, are "implied in our existence"? What incidents in your life might have led to those questions?

• How is the definition of sin as "missing the mark" or "straying from the path" different from your previous understanding of sin? Give some examples of sin from your own life that might qualify under these new definitions; give some examples of "sin" that might not.

• Describe some ways in which sins have separated you from God, and how they made you feel.

• In the metaphor of stones, what do the stones represent in your personal life? What does the backpack represent?

• What are some differences between Christianity based on guilt and Christianity based on grace? What are some examples of each from your own life?

• "The church is for sinners!" What do you think is meant by this statement?

• Do you remember a time when you repented a sin and felt your load lighten? What was the experience like?

CHAPTER TWO

# FOR BETTER, FOR WORSE

*As God's chosen ones, holy and beloved, clothe yourselves with compassion, kindness, humility, meekness, and patience. Bear with one another and, if anyone has a complaint against another, forgive each other; just as the Lord has forgiven you, so you also must forgive. Above all, clothe yourselves with love, which binds everything together in perfect harmony. And let the peace of Christ rule in your hearts, to which indeed you were called in the one body. And be thankful.*

*Colossians 3:12-15*

LaVon and I were very young when we fell in love and got married. We spent our honeymoon at the exotic La Quinta Inn in Overland Park, Kansas. Then we loaded up our U-Haul with all the furniture we'd bought at garage sales, took our entire savings—a sum of three hundred dollars—and went off to college. It was a great and wonderful adventure—for about a week.

Then, of course, reality set in. We were two human beings raised in different environments and seeing the world in different ways. Our life experiences, our physiology, our brain chemistry—everything was different. There was conflict at every turn. I confess that there were times when I looked at LaVon and said to myself, "I thought it would be easier than this."

Falling in love is easy. Staying in love for a lifetime is, for most of us, hard work. Those romantic feelings that help launch us as partners are really important, but they're not sufficient by themselves. Marriage and long-term intimate relationships are part determination, part willpower, and a constant willingness to seek out and grant forgiveness. These relationships simply cannot stand without forgiveness.

In the verses from Colossians that open this chapter, Paul describes how Christians are meant to live in community with one another. It is a passage I read at every wedding I officiate. "Clothe yourselves," Paul writes, "with compassion, kindness, humility, meekness, and patience." It's worth looking at each of these qualities individually, noting first that *clothing,* as used here, is a metaphor for our first line of response toward others.

> **Compassion:** The act of putting yourself in your partner's shoes, of feeling what he or she is feeling.
>
> **Kindness:** Performing the thoughtful acts that bless and encourage your partner, with no expectation of something in return.
>
> **Humility:** Respecting your partner as a human being and seeking to put his or her needs before your own.

**Meekness:** Gentleness. When I think of meekness, I think of Proverbs 15:15, which says, "A gentle answer turns away wrath."

**Patience:** Endurance and longsuffering; a willingness to bear with unpleasantness.

If every one of us lived up to Paul's prescription, our marriages or intimate relationships would be amazingly harmonious and blessed, and we would never *need* forgiveness. Unfortunately, most of us struggle to live these virtues on a daily basis. We don't think of the other first. We speak in harsh tones or find ourselves easily irritated. We fail to show the respect owed. Paul knows this about human nature, which is why he goes on to advise the Christians at Colossae, "Bear with one another and, if anyone has a complaint against another, forgive each other; just as the Lord has forgiven you, so you also must forgive."

I love this verse for its realism. Paul knows that no one is always going to live up to the virtues he lays out. He acknowledges that we are going to irritate each other. And so he counsels tolerance. This advice, meant for Christians living in community, is even more pertinent for Christians living in the same home in a lifelong covenant relationship. After all, even the best relationships have regular sources of conflict, many of which seem awfully petty at times.

Early in our marriage, LaVon would do our grocery shopping. (Come to think of it, she still does!) My favorite jam is strawberry, but not just any strawberry: Smucker's strawberry. But in those early years, we were struggling financially, and LaVon decided that one place she could save money was to buy the store brand of strawberry jam. Each time she came home with a Brand X strawberry jam-like product, I would say, "Why didn't you buy Smucker's? This isn't even real." She would respond, "Because they're just the same, and this brand is cheaper." I would say, "No, they're not the same. Could you please buy the good stuff next time? Here's fifty cents to cover the extra cost." Four months later, when I would finally finish the jumbo-sized jar of the store-brand jam she had bought, LaVon would come home with another giant jar of the stuff.

What a small and insignificant thing to fight about, but it captures the idea of how little things get under our skin, and it characterizes the daily conflicts in marriage. (I should add that, finally, years later, LaVon decided we made enough money to buy Smucker's!)

There are a host of little things I do that frustrate LaVon, as well. For instance, tidiness and order aren't as important to me as they are to LaVon. I spend Tuesdays at home working on my sermons. As part of the process, I spread my books and papers all over the kitchen table. When LaVon walks in after a long day at work, she will often say, "You have an office. Why are you doing this here?" At that point, I look at her with a smile and say, "Jesus needs me to do this here." That doesn't always go over very well!

Using the metaphor of stones that I introduced in the previous chapter, the strawberry jam and the papers on the kitchen table are pebbles. If we choose to hold on to all our pebbles—the irritations, the disappoint-ments, the perceived slights—then pretty soon we'll find it impossible to function. As Paul told the Colossians, no relationship can be sustained without learning to "bear with one another."

At the same time, clothing ourselves with compas-sion, kindness, humility, meekness, and patience means seeking to understand the needs of our mates and then working to meet them, in order to bless the ones we love. Over the years, I've learned that LaVon is bothered by clutter, so I try to clean up in order to bless her. For her part, LaVon has learned to accept the fact that I will never be as neat as she is, and she has agreed to buy the "good stuff" when shopping for jam.

Now let's shift metaphors from pebbles to accounting procedures. Both partners have mental ledgers for recording credits and debits, and too often in our inti-mate relationships we stop recording credits and go right on recording debits. Every time our partner does some little thing that annoys us, there's a hash mark.

"You know, you really are insensitive," we think. Check. "You're just proving that you don't care." Check. "There you go again!" Check.

If LaVon and I focused solely on the quirks that irritated us, or assumed the other was doing them out of spite, or if neither of us was willing to address the things that bothered the other, we'd be divorced by now. Instead, we do two things: we choose not to record each perceived wrong done to us by the other, and we choose to keep track of the blessings the other does for us. If the accounting procedures in your relationship are focused on keeping track of all the debits and ignoring the credits, you're doomed to a pretty miserable relationship.

So, what would happen if you just erased the debit column altogether, if you decided that, when it comes to the small stuff, you're only going to remember the positives? There are three words right at the end of our passage from Paul that are very useful here: "and be thankful." That's a key to successful long-term relationships. Choose to keep track of the blessings your partner brings into your life! A ledger that is weighted toward the positive is a big help in letting a relationship soar.

This is one of the important functions of birthdays, anniversaries, Valentine's Day, and other holidays. Despite the fact that these days often seem to exist only to sell greeting cards, when I'm writing something in those cards, it forces me to take an accounting of all the blessings LaVon has brought into my life. After I write them down, I actually *feel* more grateful for her. In one of Paul's best-loved passages, First Corinthians 13, he writes, "Love keeps no record of wrongs." When we change our accounting procedure, we begin to find more joy in our relationships.

Every night, LaVon and I pray together before she goes to bed, around 10:00 or 11:00. Then, when I come to bed at 1:00 or 2:00 a.m., I get down on my knees next to our bed to pray once more. In the darkness, I set my hands on the bed, palms uplifted, and pray. I thank God for the day. I praise him for all the blessings in my life. I pray for my kids, for our church, for our national leaders.

The last thing I do is pause and become quiet, listening to my wife breathe as she sleeps. Then I say, "God, thank you for LaVon. I'm so grateful that you blessed me with her. I pray that you would help me to love her well, and to be the husband she needs me to be."

It may have been a day when we were irritated with each other, or we may have been frustrated before she went to bad, but, somehow, when I stop and say, "Thank you, God, for blessing me with LaVon," it begins to change my heart. And I believe that over time, as I pray for God to make me the husband she needs me to be, little by little, God fulfills my desire to become a better partner.

## MEDIUM-SIZED STONES: REPENTANCE, FORGIVENESS, AND DISPOSAL

Not all stones are pocket-sized. Once we move past the thoughtlessness and passing hurts that we can learn to live with or deal with rather simply, we come to the bigger hurts—the medium-sized stones that, if left unattended, can become large. They are the things that, as Paul puts it, are not so easy to "bear with." These include neglect, hurtful words, persistent insensitivity, public embarrassments, dishonesty and deceit, and the failure to love, cherish, build up, and bless. Whereas the smaller slights create gaps that divide us, these wrongs build stone walls.

Imagine a backpack full of these larger stones—perhaps sixty pounds' worth—with the backpack strapped not to one's back, but to the chest. Carrying this load would be difficult. Now picture two people trying to embrace with such backpacks strapped to their chests. The weight of the burden would make not only breathing, talking, and walking difficult, but loving as well. The stones themselves come between us.

There are two possible responses to these bigger hurts: we can seek justice or offer mercy. If your partner never hears you ask for mercy and doesn't ever feel mercy from you, then he or she is going to seek justice, which, in this case, looks like getting even. He or she may adopt the attitude of, "You've hurt me so many times, I'm going to hurt you. I know what your needs are, but why would I meet them when you won't meet mine? I know this will hurt you, but after the way you've hurt me, you deserve it." In this way, one by one, we put stones in each other's backpack. We punish rather than love. "She gave me a rock; I'll give her two." And when we practice this "eye for an eye and tooth for a tooth" justice, we end up with two blind and toothless people inside a joyless relationship.

The answer—God's answer—is the process of forgiveness. That is the best way to let go once and for all. If we don't let go, then each slight, each harsh word, each insensitive act is saved up, and we are burdened more and more. Without forgiveness, our relationships quickly become weighed down.

So, how do we go about achieving forgiveness for these kinds of wounds within the context of a marriage or intimate relationship? Forgiveness is most freely and fully given when the one who has done the wrong repents. Repentance is a four-step process that includes awareness, regret, confession, and change.

It begins with *awareness,* our consciousness of the fact that something we've done has brought pain to our partner. In acknowledging that fact, and in doing our best to understand what our partner must feel like, we experience true *regret,* or remorse. This, too, requires time and effort. When LaVon makes me aware of something I've done wrong, I am much more likely to be defensive than remorseful. I have to think about it for a while. I have to search my heart. When I do, I find myself thinking, "I married you with a promise to love and bless you, not hurt you." I put myself in LaVon's shoes, and that's when true remorse enters the picture. It may take me a few hours or a few days, but it happens.

Some years ago, our church was in a period of activity that was especially intense. We had a capital campaign, meetings every night of the week, a new worship service that was just getting started, and several other strategic efforts underway. I was gone a lot, working on my day off, and not fully present with the family. LaVon had a part-time job and was trying to take care of our elementary-age kids. She finally sat down with me one night and said, "This is not working. I know that what you are doing is important, but I want you to imagine how you would feel if the roles were reversed, and if I were gone every night for weeks at my job and you were left with all the responsibility for the kids." The more I thought about it, the more I realized how much I would resent continuing on this path and the toll it would take on our marriage. Because of her simple question, I was able to see the situation in the light of Jesus' Golden Rule: I was not treating LaVon the way I would want to be treated. The longer I thought about her question, the more remorse I felt.

Once we are aware of the stone we've placed in the other's backpack, and we've begun to understand the impact it has had, we're ready for *confession,* which sounds something like this: "I think I finally understand how you were affected by what I did, and I'm very sorry. I didn't mean to hurt you, but I realize that I did. Would you please forgive me?" Don't use the opportunity to point out your partner's faults; that's not confession. Neither is a quick, mumbled "Sorry." Either of these approaches simply puts more stones in your partner's backpack. This is about acknowledging the wrong you've done and earnestly asking for grace.

Most of us are capable of adopting or improving in these first three steps of repentance: awareness, regret, and confession. It's the fourth step, *change,* that often trips us up. And yet this is the most important step. In the Greek New Testament, the word for *repentance* is *metanoia* (and several other related words). It means "to change one's mind and one's heart, leading to a change in behavior." If sin is stepping off the path God intends, repentance is returning to the right path. True repentance is not simply feeling bad about what you did and asking for forgiveness, although those steps are essential as well. You've also got to commit to change.

Can you guarantee—to the partner you've wronged or to God—that you're never going to do this or that thing again? Probably not. But you can say that you understand the harm you've caused and that you're going to do your best never to it again. And both parties in a close relationship are most likely going to keep coming back with confessions about the faults they have difficulty overcoming.

This process of repentance promotes healing. In the awareness stage, we recognize the burden our partner is carrying as a wound that we caused. Repentance involves removing the burden caused by our sin—taking the stones from our partner's backpack, and from our own backpack as well. Lifting these burdens contributes to the healing of both parties and allows for real change to occur. Of course, once repentance is extended, the question then becomes whether the other party will forgive. Sometimes we don't feel like forgiving, but we decide to do so anyway, knowing that at some point we are going to need forgiveness ourselves. Part of forgiveness is sheer willpower, a hard-won decision to go through with the process. One woman wrote to me and said, "I find that husbands are a lot like kids. It's when you want to love them or forgive them the least that you need to do it the most. I find that when I make up my mind to stop being bitter or annoyed at my husband that our love is the best. *It's all in what I make up my mind to do.*"

Because we are human, all of us sometimes do things we shouldn't do. When your partner has done everything or, more realistically, almost everything possible to take the pain away, to lift the rocks from your backpack, then it's up to you. Sometimes we decide that we like to collect these old rocks. We hear our partner earnestly seek our forgiveness, but we decide to hold on to the rock. We decide that we like it in our backpack. At that point, the offended becomes the offender. You become responsible for the wall between you. That's no better or fairer than creating it in the first place. Both repentance and forgiveness take effort. Yet both are works and expressions of love.

# THE MOST SERIOUS KINDS OF SINS

That brings us to the most serious sins people can commit against a mate, grievances so serious they tear at the soul of the other person and represent a serious threat to the relationship. Examples that come to mind include serious and persistent deceit; physical, psychological, or verbal abuse; addictions; and infidelity. These are each like forty-pound boulders. It's not possible to carry a stone like that for long.

Like all sins, these serious grievances require awareness, remorse, confession, and change, but the deep pain caused may require more time in the remorse and confession stages. Be aware that, for both parties, these grievances usually involve deep-seated issues that make it very hard to change without help from counselors, support groups, or other such experiences that promote intentional and serious soul work. It is possible for healing, forgiveness, and reconciliation to occur, but this is far from a foregone conclusion.

There are exceptions, however. For example, there are those who suggest that God requires the wronged party to stay in an abusive or deceit-filled marriage. I don't believe this. Marriage was not meant to be a life sentence or a time of torture; neither were our homes meant to be places of fear. A marriage filled with persistent deceit, addictions, or abuse has ceased to be a marriage as God intends. Marriages can survive these serious sins, provided there is real and substantial change, but even then, they cannot do so without grace. I've known many who overcame these sins and whose marriages were healed. But I've also known many whose marriages were unable to survive, largely because the abuser, deceiver, or addict was unable to set aside the boulder, continuing to place it back in the partner's arms by reverting to the sinful behavior.

A more common form of serious sin in marriage and committed relationships is infidelity. In an anonymous survey of the congregation I serve, 8.1 percent of married people had been unfaithful at some point in their lives. The number was lower for couples in their twenties and thirties, and went up the longer a couple was married.

Many relationships simply cannot withstand the aftermath of the discovery of adultery—and generally it is discovered. That's why even Jesus, who spoke out so strongly against divorce, made an exception in the case of adultery. In Matthew 5:32, he said, "But I say to you that whoever divorces his wife except for sexual unfaithfulness forces her to commit adultery." Jesus did not *prescribe* divorce in the event of infidelity, but he did allow it, recognizing how hard it is to heal a relationship after a breach of trust this great. I am confident Jesus would have said the same thing about physical and psychological abuse.

I can say, as a pastor, that violations of marriage vows have so many variables and require such extraordinary grace that they cannot always be healed. Still, I've seen amazing healing that has happened in marriages touched by infidelity. I once asked a group of congregants and friends about their experiences with infidelity, and I received twenty-two single-spaced pages of responses! Half of these marriages did not survive the affair. Surprisingly, though, half of them did.

Those whose relationships did survive an affair described the process they went through and the pain they experienced, and detailed the amazing mercy that the wronged spouses were able to show. Some of those spouses actually were able to say at the end of their letters, "Pastor Adam, it's really surprising, but in the years since, we've discovered a love we never knew before." In many cases, the marriages had become stronger than they had ever been. That's grace.

One of the letters, from a woman who was still working through the process of healing and forgiving, captured what many others noted:

> I wasn't sure at first that I wanted to forgive my husband, but I decided to try. It helped that he admitted to the affair and said he wanted to work to rebuild our marriage. I thought at first that I should forgive him because it was the "right" and "Christian" thing to do, but at the same

time, I argued with myself that I should walk away because it hurt too much.

There wasn't a moment when I could say, "Okay, now I've forgiven him." Forgiving him was something that I had to decide to do daily, and it got easier over time. I don't think that my forgiving him was necessarily only for his sake. I needed to forgive him for my sake as well, because if I didn't, my bitterness, hurt, and anger would have stayed in control of my actions and emotions.

Besides forgiveness, we had to rebuild trust. In the very beginning, I wanted to know when "it" wouldn't hurt anymore and when I wouldn't think about it all the time, every day. And again, there wasn't a point in time that I could mark when it didn't hurt as much or when I wasn't thinking about it as much, but over time it subsided.

Therapy was another thing that helped get us through, because we realized that the problem was not the affair itself. That was only the presenting symptom of some underlying problems in our relationship. I think that was key to me being able to eventually forgive—the realization that although the affair wasn't my fault, I was at fault for some of the problems with our relationship.

That couple is still in the process of healing, something that doesn't happen overnight. It takes a willingness to practice repentance and forgiveness, as well as a great deal of time to reestablish trust. It is the role of the offender to do everything possible to bear the burden *with* the wounded mate. If you feel the weight of that burden, if you acknowledge and confess it honestly and openly, and if you are committed never to violate the covenant again, then your relationship may have a fighting chance. Until your partner can set aside the boulder they carry from the affair, your task is to help them carry it. You will struggle, wondering when they will finally forgive. They will eventually be ready for you to help them set aside the boulder. But this is not something people get over in a week or a month. You will increase the likelihood of success with counseling, and with a sincere turn toward God. Trying to heal a breach like this without turning to God for support and in repentance will be infinitely more difficult. You'll need to help your partner carry that stone until you've taken it away, until you are carrying it. When your partner is finally able to let it go, it's not that he or she has forgotten it, but has chosen no longer to think about it.

If you are the one who has been wronged, whether or not the relationship survives, at some point you have to put the boulder down. If you don't, it will affect everything you do. At some point, you've got to *choose* to let go and give it to God.

## GRACE FOR THE SINNER

There is something else to be said to the one who was unfaithful: infidelity is not the unpardonable sin. I got another note, this one from a man:

> As a person who ruined his marriage with infidelity, I can tell you that the pain never ends.... Every day I am haunted by the actions that I took. At times I can feel for-giveness, and at other times I still cannot believe what a terrible person I was. I know that God forgives even the

worst of offenses, but I still have trouble forgiving myself.
I pray for forgiveness every day and for the people I hurt
the most.

This man had carried the boulder of guilt for five
long years. This is not God's intention. The consequences of our sin may lead our life down a different
path, but there is always grace for the sinner. God seeks
true repentance—awareness, remorse, confession, and
change—and with that repentance come healing and
grace. God is the God of the second chance. You may
not save your relationship, but you can find life and joy
again as you bring those heavy, heavy stones to God in
a spirit of repentance.

## SIX IMPORTANT WORDS TO MAKE
## MARRIAGE LAST

As mentioned in the preface, there are six words
that must be said regularly if a marriage or intimate

relationship is to last—two sets of three words each. Sometimes you'll say the first three and your mate the second three. Sometimes your mate will start, and you will finish. But your relationship is hopeless without freely sharing these words:

I am sorry.

I forgive you.

Based on the survey at our church, 92 percent of marriages will not face the issue of adultery. Most will not face abusive situations or addiction, though these are possibilities in all of our lives. All couples, however, will need to decide what to do with the thousands of pebbles tossed their way each year by their mates. Generally we bear with each other, and, as we learn what irritates our mates, we seek, in compassion, kindness, humility, meekness, and patience, to refrain from doing these things. And as we mature in our love, we learn to change our accounting systems, keeping track of the credits while setting aside the debits.

All of us have times when we wound the other, intentionally or unintentionally, in more significant ways that the person simply can't "bear with." Here, repentance becomes critical. We become aware of how our actions have wounded the other, we express remorse, and we commit to change. When the other has wronged us, we choose to forgive not just seven times, but seventy times seven times. And once we forgive, we don't go dredging up past sins.

When the wrongs are of the most serious kind—the forty-pound boulders—time will be needed for healing and regaining trust. These wrongs likely will require the help of a counselor.

If you are the one who has sinned, know that you'll need to demonstrate sincere repentance and then help your mate carry the burden of hurt they will bear for a time. Consider writing a letter to your mate, beginning with a sincere apology and ending with a list of the blessings you find in him or her.

Whether you are the sinner or the one sinned against, your daily prayer might sound something like this:

"Lord, thank you for my partner, for my spouse. Help us to love each other, and teach us to receive that love." If you're carrying around wounds long since past, or if you have the habit of dredging up past sins, you might make this your prayer: "God, please help me to forgive. Give me the strength I need. Help me to let it go."

And here's a prayer we can all pray: "Oh, God, help us to forgive others as we seek your forgiveness. God, help us to be reconciled in our relationships and faithful to them. Heal us, we pray, and restore to us the joy of your salvation. In the name of the one who gave his life for our forgiveness, amen."

## THINKING IT THROUGH

• For each of the five qualities Paul lists in Colossians—compassion, kindness, humility, meekness, and patience—think of an example (positive or negative) from relationships you have experienced, and imagine the alternatives.

• Do you think forgiveness needs to be thought of or handled differently in a marriage or intimate relationship than in other relationships? Why or why not?

• Think of a stone you've placed in your mate's backpack. In the spaces below, write out briefly the steps you took or could have taken at each stage of forgiveness:

Awareness

Regret

Confession

Change

• In cases where you haven't been able to change, how did you feel? How do you think your mate felt? How do you think God felt? Have any of the participants' feelings changed over time, and if so, how?

• "Marriage was not meant to be a life sentence." Reflect on this sentence. What thoughts does it call to mind? Do you agree? Why or why not?

• What are some sins that you would be able to "bear with"? What are some sins that you wouldn't? For you, what's the dividing line?

# CHAPTER THREE

# SEVENTY TIMES SEVEN

*Then Peter came and said to him, "Lord, if another member of the church sins against me, how often should I forgive? As many as seven times?" Jesus said to him, "Not seven times, but, I tell you, seventy times seven."*

*Matthew 18:21-22*

*So when you are offering your gift at the altar, if you remember that your brother or sister has something against you, leave your gift there before the altar and go; first be reconciled to your brother or sister, and then come and offer your gift.*

*Matthew 5:23-24*

When I was in high school I sold women's shoes at the mall. One day while I was working, I approached two women whose backs were to me. I greeted them and offered my assistance, asking if they needed anything. They ignored me. As a sales clerk, I was used to rudeness, but it really bothered me that they did not even acknowledge my words. I decided I would stand back at the counter. If they wanted something, they would have to come seek me out. There I stood, nursing the thought that they had snubbed me. A moment later, one of the women turned and started speaking to her friend in sign language. Neither of these women could hear. They had not ignored my offer of help, because they had never heard it. It was I, not they, who had been rude.

Often the little hurts that we feel, or that others feel because of us, are only false perceptions and misunderstandings. Last week, I went out of turn at a four-way stop. As I pulled through the intersection, the person to my right, whose turn it was to go, laid into her horn.

I did not mean to go out of turn. I was tired and hadn't even noticed she was there before I was. When she honked her horn, I found that I was irritated.

"Really, lady," I thought, "you have to honk your horn at me for that? Have you never accidentally gone out of turn before?"

Every day, we gather pebbles—lots of pebbles. They raise our blood pressure, create frustration, and head our day off in the wrong direction. What are we to do?


## PEBBLES


In dealing with pebbles, we can decide not to, in the words of Richard Carlson's excellent little book, "sweat the small stuff" (*Don't Sweat the Small Stuff—and It's All Small Stuff* [(New York: Hyperion, 1997]). We can regularly practice the art of letting the little things go. But how do we do that? How do we avoid holding on to the anger or irritation or resentment that comes from the pebbles thrown at us each day? And how often do we need to forgive these acts?

Peter asked a similar question in the Scripture passage at the beginning of this chapter. He asked, "Lord, if another member of the church sins against me, how often should I forgive? Seven times?"

Note here that when Peter referred to "the church," it consisted primarily of his brother Andrew, his friends James and John, and a handful of others. Peter was asking, in essence, "Lord, if Andrew or James wrongs me, how often do I need to forgive them? Is seven times enough, Lord? I'm on six and I'm hoping seven is all that I owe them."

Jesus surprised Peter by answering, "No, not seven times, but seventy times seven times," an idiomatic phrase that meant, in essence, an infinite number of times.

Jesus was telling Peter, and through Peter each of us, that we are to let go of our right to hold on to these pebbles, and even the bigger rocks. Our lives are meant to be characterized by grace and forgiveness. Jesus was asking us to say, "You've wronged me and I could hold on to my anger, demanding some kind of satisfaction, but I choose instead to let it go and not hold it against you any longer."

I'm guessing that if each of us held on to every little irritant, slight, and perceived wrong, within a few days, we could easily wind up with more gravel than a person can carry. Often, others aren't even aware that we feel they have wronged us. They don't know to ask forgiveness. So, somewhere along the way we've got to find the capacity to let go. But how do we do that? For these little slights, I suggest three steps captured by the acronym RAP.

The first step is to *remember* your own shortcomings, the little sins you regularly commit. When you feel that somebody has offended you, stop and consider how many times you've done something like it. When someone cuts me off in traffic and I feel a twinge of irritation, I remember the times I've done it myself, and my frustration disappears. It's difficult to stay mad at somebody else when you're conscious of your own flaws.

Recently, on an evening flight back to Kansas City, the flight attendant seemed unusually grumpy. She was short with passengers. She barked the orders to turn off phones and electronics. Her demeanor set others on edge, including me. My first reaction was, "She needs to work on her people skills. I'm surprised they have her on a flight like this." But in the midst of mentally condemning her poor people skills, I remembered another trip when I had been short with someone else. I had been tired and in a hurry, and I was rude. I didn't mean to be. It didn't reflect who I hope to be or who I think I really am.

When I remembered my own recent failure at kindness, compassion, and patience, I found I was much more gracious toward our flight attendant, which led me to the second step in letting go of the little things: *assume* the best of the person who has slighted you.

I began imagining what may have caused the flight attendant to be so impatient and grumpy. I wondered if she had a child sick at home, or if she wasn't feeling well. I imagined she might be working overtime and was just very tired. That led me to the third step in letting go of the little things. I did what Jesus told us to do for those who may not treat us well. He told us to *pray* for them and to love them. The Apostle Paul, quoting the Proverbs, told us not to return evil for evil, but to return blessing instead. I began to pray for my flight attendant: "Lord, you know what her circumstances are. She seems particularly stressed, tired, or at the end of her rope. Please bless her, and use me to bless her."

As I began to pray for the flight attendant, an interesting thing happened. In my heart, I felt compassion for her and wanted to bless her. When she finally came to my seat and asked what I wanted to drink, I felt prompted to tell her, "I want you to know how grateful I am for you and for the way you serve us. Your job really matters, and you make our flight easier." She paused, taken aback, and then she smiled and said, "It's been a hectic day, and it seems I've had one complaint after another. You're the first person to thank me in a long time. I really appreciate that." For the rest of the flight, she was a different person. All she had needed was one person to show kindness, and she was able to let go of the frustration and stress she'd been feeling all day. Before I got off the plane, she thanked me again for my encouraging words.

Once you begin practicing the RAP method a lot, it can almost become a game—assuming the best of those who throw pebbles at you and finding ways to return blessings. In the process, you can avoid being caught up in anger or irritation, and, every once in a while, the blessings you return might just have a remarkable impact on the pebble thrower.

Just RAP: *remember* your own shortcomings, *assume* the best of people, and *pray* for them.

## MEDIUM AND LARGE STONES: REPENTANCE REQUIRED

Practicing the process of RAP when someone throws small pebbles at us usually works. But what if the wounds are more serious and the rocks larger? A friend has betrayed your trust, a co-worker has lied about you, a business associate has cheated you, or you've otherwise been seriously wronged by another. We know that forgiveness is the only way forward; otherwise the anger and resentment will only build and build. Yet we struggle with the idea of forgiveness in these situations, often asking a host of questions about what it means to forgive.

I conducted an informal survey of the people in my congregation, requesting they submit questions about forgiving those who had wronged them. I received more than eighty replies. Below, I share a few of the most frequently asked questions, along with my thoughts about each.

*Is forgiving the same thing as condoning?*

No, forgiveness is not the same as condoning. Forgiveness means letting go of the right to retribution. We are letting go of the pain in our own lives and putting down the stones we have carried in our hearts. Yet we are also putting down the stones we might have thrown at those who wronged us. Having said that, we can, and usually must, choose to let go of these stones, while still being clear that what happened was not okay. We are choosing not to allow these wrongs to continue to affect us. We are choosing not to give the wrongdoer any more power over us.

*Does forgiving dismiss the consequences?*

Often forgiveness means setting aside the right to retribution, but sometimes there are consequences that cannot be avoided. If someone lies to you or betrays a confidence, you may forgive that person, but it may be a long time before you trust the person again. This loss of trust is a consequence people face by virtue of their dishonesty or betrayal, even though you may have forgiven them.

When my children were small and they did something that required punishment, we would put them in time-out. As they got a little older, we would ground them. At some point during the punishment, one of my daughters, Danielle or Rebecca, might say, "Dad, I'm really sorry. I know I did the wrong thing. I shouldn't have done that."

And I'd say to her, "Thank you for saying that. I love you so much. I understand, and it's all right now."

"Am I still grounded?"

"Yes, honey, I'm sorry. You're still grounded."

Her being grounded was not retribution; it was a way of teaching her and forming her character so that she would avoid repeating the transgression in the future. Forgiving my daughter was a way of restoring our relationship. Both punishment and forgiveness were essential to her development, and they were not mutually exclusive ideas.

If the aim of a punishment is only retribution, then this punishment must be set aside once forgiveness enters the picture. But if the aim of a punishment is redemption, then that punishment may be essential, even after forgiveness happens. God works through consequences and punishment. Punishment can be important not only for teaching the individual, but also for maintaining order in society. It is possible to forgive someone who has committed a crime against you, while still feeling that society, and perhaps the redemption of the individual, is best served by incarceration.

*Do we forgive someone who has done something serious and who hasn't repented or asked for forgiveness?*

Once again, the answer can be both yes and no. If we're talking about pebbles, we must routinely forgive even when the other doesn't repent. Sometimes people don't understand that they've done wrong. Sometimes they are not even aware of what happened.

Some pebbles can become more serious, and we must confront the one who has wronged us, even though the issue is minor, to keep it from becoming bigger. Typically, though, we let go of the pebbles and offer forgiveness without waiting for repentance on the part of the person who wronged us. We do this as much for ourselves as for the offender, and, in the process, become grateful that others routinely forgive us.

But what about larger stones? Do we forgive these

more serious wrongs when the other has not displayed an awareness of the wrong, expressed regret, asked for forgiveness, or expressed a willingness to change? Here, it is important to remember that there are two dimensions to forgiveness: there is your internal release of bitterness, anger, or desire for revenge, and there is the extension of mercy toward the one who has wronged you.

Regarding your release of anger, bitterness, and desire for revenge, you must forgive. The more serious the wound, the longer the process may take. But failure to forgive in this sense gives power to the one who wronged you. It is you, not they, who are hurt by your unwillingness to forgive. You continue to carry the stones in the "backpack" of your heart, and they rob you of life, joy, and peace.

In the second dimension of forgiveness—extending mercy to those who have wronged us—we may actually harm wrongdoers if we extend mercy too quickly. Wrestling with the hurt they have caused is a part of their redemptive process, and for Christians, redemption should always be the goal.

In December of 1997, fourteen-year-old Michael Carneal walked into the lobby of his high school in Paducah, Kentucky, and began shooting at a group of teenagers who had gathered early to pray. He killed three of those classmates and wounded four.

A day or two later, some students there did something they thought Jesus wanted them to do. With the national spotlight on them, they made up a sign that said, "Michael, we forgive you."

Yes, Jesus tells us to forgive, but at that point, Michael wasn't asking for anybody's forgiveness. Offering him mercy did not help. Of course, those students would eventually need to let go of the hate and bitterness in their hearts, but extending mercy so quickly to one who had not asked for it, who had not repented, who had done something so terrible was surely not what Jesus had in mind. In fact, their actions could well have stopped the redemption process. Michael needed to come to terms with the terrible weight of what he had done. He needed to feel the horror of it, to confess and be changed because of it. Once that happened, it might have been appropriate to show mercy to him, although even mercy would not have waived the consequences of such an act.

Offering mercy before a person understands the need for it can diminish the gravity of the act. It gets in the way of the true goal of forgiveness, which is the redemption of the other person.

I am reminded of a domestic violence workshop I attended. Often, after the first time an abuser beats his spouse (in most cases domestic violence is committed by men, though not always), the abuser feels terrible remorse. He is apologetic and swears it will never happen again. He seems to have repented. The spouse takes him back, often, if the abused is a Christan, believing that this is what Christians are supposed to do. Then, in many cases, a week or a month later, he abuses again. He feels bad again, and she may show mercy once more.

But mercy doesn't bring change. Instead, the victim has become an inadvertent enabler of abuse. The cycle of violence, remorse, and mercy develops a rhythm, and suddenly it's a pattern. That's what can happen if mercy is extended when it should not have been.

The New Testament calls people to repentance so they may receive forgiveness. Let's look again at the four basic components of repentance: *awareness* of the wrong done, *regret* for the pain and harm caused, *confession* and a request for forgiveness and restoration, and *change,* or a real effort to avoid committing the wrong again.

While it is generally true that we don't extend the gift of mercy before earnest repentance happens, there are exceptions to this rule. There are times when extending mercy before repentance actually leads to shame and guilt on the part of the one who has wronged us, and moves them toward genuine repentance. The greatest example of this is Jesus and his death on the cross. From the cross, he prays, "Father, forgive them, for they know not what they do." Such a magnificent act of mercy would haunt those who heard his prayer for the rest of their lives. Even now, two thousand years later, we look at this scene and it moves us to repentance.

This practice of offering mercy and kindness to those who don't deserve it, and the power this has to change others, permeates the New Testament. Jesus taught his disciples to love their enemies and pray for those who persecute. He taught his followers to forgive.

## A BIBLICAL PROCESS FOR RECONCILIATION

In Matthew 18, Jesus assumed there would be times of conflict in the community he was forming, which was the church. He knew his followers would sin against one another. So he gave advice for how Christians should seek reconciliation. He had already spoken of this in Matthew 5:23-24, as part of the Sermon on the Mount: "So when you are offering your gift at the altar,

if you remember that your brother or sister has something against you, leave your gift there before the altar
and go; first be reconciled to your brother or sister, and
then come and offer your gift."

Keep in mind that Jesus was speaking in Galilee, and
the altar was in Jerusalem at the temple. He was saying,
"After you've made your way to Jerusalem, which is a
ten-day journey, if you realize that you've neglected to
seek the forgiveness of someone you have wronged back
home, before offering your sacrifice to God, travel back
and make amends, then travel ten days once again to
offer your sacrifice to God." This teaching was delivered
in the tradition of hyperbole, with which Jesus often addressed his followers—in other words, it was given in
terms that were practically absurd (for example, "cut off
your hand" or "pluck out your eye") to point out an important idea. In this case, Jesus was using hyperbole to
say that a right relationship with God requires that we
make amends with our neighbors whom we have
wronged. This is part of Christian discipleship, that we

initiate the process of reconciliation when we've wronged someone, or even just when they *feel* we've wronged them.

Our failure to make amends with those we have wronged, or with those who perceive that we have wronged them, affects our relationship with God. Is there someone in your life who feels you've wronged them? Do you need to contact them today and seek to make amends?

In Matthew 18, Jesus went on to tell his disciples that if someone else wronged them and the other person did not come forward to make amends, it was the disciples' responsibility to initiate reconciliation:

> If another member of the church sins against you, go and point out the fault when the two of you are alone. If the member listens to you, you have regained that one. But if you are not listened to, take one or two others along with you, so that every word may be confirmed by the evidence of two or three witnesses. If the member refuses to listen to them, tell it to the church; and if the offender

refuses to listen even to the church, let such a one be to you as a Gentile and a tax collector. (Matthew 18:15-17)

Remember that when Jesus spoke of the church, he was referring to a rather small group. He was saying, "Peter, when John says or does something that wounds you, if he doesn't see it or acknowledge it, go and speak to him in private and tell him." Jesus' admonition had two parts: we are to initiate reconciliation, not waiting for the other; and we are not to tell all our friends about the wound inflicted upon us by another, but instead are to speak with them alone.

How different this is from the way many Christians address being wronged in their lives today. Too often, if others don't notice the wrong they've committed, or don't believe they've done anything wrong, we don't have the nerve to sit down and talk with them. Instead, we tell our entire group about the other's sin. Perhaps we share it on social media. When we do this, we make reconciliation even harder, but more than that, we now have sinned against the other, and often our sin is worse than the sin committed against us to begin with!

Jesus went on to offer a second and third suggestion about what to do if the one who has sinned against you fails to acknowledge it. (We can assume these are not small slights or pebbles that we can routinely let go.) Jesus said that if the other doesn't hear or acknowledge what we're saying, then we return to speak to this person with two trusted friends whose job is to listen, bear witness to the supposed wrong, and help bring about reconciliation, which is the goal of the entire process. Finally, if the person does not accept the witness of these friends and instead persists in sin, then the church (at that time a group of perhaps twelve to twenty) appeals to the individual to repent and be reconciled to the one wronged. If the person still refuses to repent and reconcile, then that person is to be treated like a "Gentile and a tax collector."

This entire process described by Jesus is sometimes referred to as *church discipline.* The last proscription, to treat the offender as a Gentile or tax collector, is interesting. In some churches, this command has been interpreted as excommunication. But it is helpful to remember that Jesus spent much of his time with Gentiles and tax collectors. He loved them, enjoyed fellowship with them, healed their sick, and invited them to be his followers. Seen in this light, it appears that Jesus was instructing the church to treat the offender as they would treat anyone else who needed his grace and love. The other may have broken fellowship because of an unwillingness to repent and be reconciled, but it doesn't make that person an enemy, just one to whom the church would continue to reach out and draw to Christ.

In this book, we've talked about forgiving others when they wrong us, and seeking forgiveness and making amends when we've wronged someone else. In the two passages from Matthew's gospel, from chapters 5 and 18, we clearly see that both sides of the forgiveness equation are part of Christian discipleship.

So once again, I ask you: is there someone who has

wronged you and, in so doing, has erected a wall between the two of you? If there is, God may be calling you to reach out to that person and explain your feelings in an attempt to be reconciled.

Several years ago, I said something from the pulpit that proved hurtful to a couple in our congregation. I was telling a story about them, trying to be humorous and to make a point about our need to welcome others, but my comments wounded the couple. I did not even know whom the story was about, as it had been passed on to me by someone else. But I had not gotten the details of the story exactly right, nor did I cite the right motives. Some months later, a couple in the church came to me and said they were the ones I had spoken of and that my comments had hurt them. When they explained the background of the story, it was clear I had misinterpreted their actions. More than that, it was clear I had been in the wrong in sharing the story.

It is, of course, difficult to hear people say that you've hurt them. Your defenses immediately go up. But how grateful I was that the couple took seriously Matthew 18 and came to me rather than holding on to the wrong, allowing it to become a wall between us and possibly leading them to leave the church. Instead, because they came forward, I was genuinely able to repent. I became aware of the impact my actions had on someone else, I felt tremendous remorse, I confessed and asked for forgiveness, and I pledged not to do the same thing again. In fact, their actions taught me an important lesson that would keep me from hurting others in the future. Their decision to follow Matthew 18 turned out to be healing for them and redemptive for me.

## THE REALLY BIG STONES: CHIPPING AWAY, A LITTLE AT A TIME

Most of the sins others commit against us are pebbles. Some are like the medium-sized stones that wound but that, with time, we eventually move beyond. But there are some wounds others inflict that are so deep they cannot be forgiven quickly. The impact of these wounds can be devastating, and letting go of them takes time, remarkable grace, and the help of others.

One New Year's Eve, the son of one of our church members went to a party at a Kansas nightclub with some young adults, including his roommate. Afterward, a group went back to the son's apartment. There, the young man and his roommate got into a fight, and someone called the son's brother to come and help break it up. The brother came and stopped the roommate. The roomate went to his bedroom, returned with a gun, and shot and killed the young man's brother. The young man held his brother in his arms as he died.

The roommate was tried and sentenced to prison. Meanwhile, the father, our church member, faced tremendous grief from the loss of his son. The anger and pain formed a boulder chained to his soul. There was no way he could drag it around by himself. He had to decide whether to let his son's death also kill his own spirit or whether to find some way to let go of the anger, resentment, and pain.

It took time for the father to let go, but eventually he found the resentment giving way to grace. I asked him how he did it. He said, "I had to surrender and ask God through my tears, my pain, and my sorrow, 'Help me. Help me make something good come from this horrible, evil act. Help me to do something that will honor you and my son's memory.'"

Over time, the father began to let go of the right to retribution. He prayed over and over and over again, not only for healing, but for his son's killer. He tried to see the roommate as another human being, as another father's son. He tried to assume that the roommate wasn't entirely bad, but someone who, that night, had made a terribly bad decision.

"God is still completing this process," he told me, "and will continue to help me work through this, I suppose, until I go home to be reunited with my son."

The father now volunteers to work with prisoners.

He has shared his story of pain with hundreds of prisoners, telling them how, through Christ, he learned to let go of the hate and resentment, and is still letting go today.

This kind of wound does not disappear after a day. I picture the boulder being chipped away, a little at a time. The hope is that, one day, by the grace of God, the stone will be sculpted by God and the work of friends and family into something redemptive and beautiful. In the case of our church member, that redemption looks like a man whose pain led to his profound witness to prisoners, which, in turn, has touched hundreds of men's lives.

Each of us has hurt somebody else. Somebody is carrying rocks with our names on them in their backpack. If you can think of a person like that, why not acknowledge your wrong-doing and express your remorse? Why not ask forgiveness? Pray for the strength and courage to do that, and to have the right words to express your sorrow. Even if the other doesn't forgive you, it will help you both.

And if there is someone whose stones you've been carrying around, someone toward whom you feel bitterness and the desire for retaliation, perhaps now is the time to let go, or at least to try placing that person in the hands of God, allowing God to be responsible for justice. It's time for you to trust and to let it go. Pray for God to bless and heal the other and to give you the strength to forgive.

We all need healing and reconciliation in our lives. It takes willingness and work, but the rewards are huge. And on the other side of the process is freedom, for you and for others, as well as joy in walking the path God has laid before us.

# THINKING IT THROUGH

• Think of a simple, everyday slight that you experienced recently. How did you handle it? Do you think you should have handled it differently? If so, how?

• For the slight above, think through the RAP process and write what each step below might have entailed.

**R**emember your own shortcomings

**A**ssume the best of the person

**P**ray for the person

• Here are three difficult questions about forgiveness. Briefly write the answers you would give:

Is forgiving the same as condoning?

Does forgiving dismiss the consequences?

Do we forgive someone who has done something serious and who hasn't repented or asked for forgiveness?

• Look over Jesus' reconciliation process described in this chapter. Using some of the same concepts, suggest a reconciliation process for family or for work.

• If you can, put yourself in the place of the father in the story of the young man who was killed. How would you feel? Would you ever be able to forgive? If you would, how long do you think it might take?

# CHAPTER FOUR

# THE DREAMCOAT

*Realizing that their father was dead, Joseph's brothers said, "What if Joseph still bears a grudge against us and pays us back in full for all the wrong that we did to him?" So they approached Joseph, saying, "Your father gave this instruction before he died, 'Say to Joseph: I beg you, forgive the crime of your brothers and the wrong they did in harming you.' Now therefore please forgive the crime of the servants of the God of your father." Joseph wept when they spoke to him. Then his brothers also wept, fell down before him, and said, "We are here as your slaves." But Joseph said to them, "Do not be afraid! Am I in the place of God? Even though you intended to do harm to me, God intended it for good, in order to preserve a numerous people, as he is doing today. So have no fear; I myself will provide for you and your little ones." In this way he reassured them, speaking kindly to them. Genesis 50:15-21*

## JOSEPH'S STORY: PART ONE

Joseph did not have perfect parents or grandparents or great-grandparents. In fact, his was a family that would have kept a team of therapists busy for several lifetimes. Their story, and it is quite a story, is spread out over most of Genesis. Within this sprawling and convoluted tale is the first use in the Bible of the word at the core of this book, *forgive,* and the family was certainly in need of it. Their story has a great deal to teach us about how we come to forgive and what God can do with the pain we cause one another.

The story begins with Joseph's great-grandparents, Abraham and Sarah, who set the unpleasantness in motion by sending Sarah's stepson Ishmael away so that their son Isaac could be the favored child. This conflict is still seen in the relationship between the spiritual descendants of Ishmael and Isaac, the Muslims and the Jews.

Isaac married Rebecca, who gave birth to twins

named Esau and Jacob. Isaac loved Esau, but Rebecca loved Jacob, and this led to a great deal of manipulation and intrigue as Rebecca and her favored son deceived Isaac and cheated Esau out of his birthright. When Jacob married sisters Leah and Rachel and began having children with them and their maidservants, Bilhah and Zilpah, it's not a complete surprise that he followed the long-standing family tradition of picking a favorite child of his own.

That child was Joseph, who went from Bible to Broadway in the Andrew Lloyd Webber and Tim Rice musical *Joseph and the Amazing Technicolor Dreamcoat.* Joseph may have had three generations of Israeli patriarchs as his immediate ancestors, but their faith and God's blessings did not make his family fully functional—and they did not make his life easy. Being the favorite was a decidedly mixed blessing.

Joseph's story does make it easier to accept that none of us had the perfect parents. There are no perfect parents, just as there are no perfect children or siblings. You didn't have them. Neither did I. (But I'm still grateful for you, Mom and Dad!)

Joseph, though, did get special treatment, and at one point he received from his father an extraordinarily beautiful and expensive multicolored coat. His father told his brothers and sister what a special child Joseph was, which of course was just the thing they wanted to hear. In turn, Joseph, tone deaf to their resentment, shared dreams he'd had in which his brothers bowed down before him. He didn't know what the dreams meant, but they did seem to indicate that he was really something and that his brothers were, well, not so much.

The brothers' anger built up until one day, when Joseph approached as the brothers were tending their sheep in the fields, one of the boys suggested that they kill their obnoxious brother. They all decided this was a pretty good idea. That agreement in itself was a powerful testament to the level of pain and dysfunction within the family.

Fortunately, one of the brothers said, "Wait a minute.

Let's not kill him. There's a Midianite slave-trading caravan right over there. Maybe they'd buy him from us. We'll make some money, he'll wind up a slave, and we can tell Dad he was eaten by a wild animal. He'll be out of our hair for good."

And so Joseph was betrayed by his family. He was just a kid, maybe ten or twelve years old, and his own brothers sold him into slavery. They ripped his coat and dipped it in goat blood and told their father that Joseph had been mauled and eaten by wild beasts. Their father's heart was broken, and Joseph wound up in Egypt.

Joseph and Jacob had both dumped medium-sized stones on Joseph's brothers—a lot of them. The coat. The praise. The bragging. The dream. The brothers' reaction to all those medium-sized stones was to give Joseph a huge stone, and nearly a tombstone. Joseph had to endure years of slavery in Egypt and then a false accusation that sent him to prison. For most of us, the last thing on our minds, if imprisoned in a foreign country, would be love for our brothers. Instead, we would stack the stones around us in that cell, cursing the day our brothers had put us there. And no doubt Joseph held on to rocks too big to lift, let alone carry. But his story was not over.

## PEBBLES

We've been using the image of a backpack to represent our souls, and stones as the weight we carry because of the wrongs done to us or the wrongs we have done to others. There are stones of all sizes, and family members give and take them just as everyone else does. In fact, given the tight quarters and close relationships, it's not surprising that families can have more than their share.

Can you think of ways your parents disappointed you, or ways their actions hurt you? Some of you reading this book may struggle to think of any. Others are immediately seized with painful memories of physical or emotional abuse. Most of us can remember some disappointments and pain but also have an appreciation for blessings received from our parents. Joseph undoubtedly was grateful that Jacob had loved him so much, and after years of reflection probably realized that his father's love and behavior patterns had both positively and negatively shaped his life story.

What about your parents or siblings? Did they inflict wounds that you still carry with you, or wounds you've forgiven but will never forget? And what would they say about you? Do their backpacks contain any stones with your name on them?

We've all got pebbles that our family members have tossed our way. Some may have seemed like boulders at the time, and only in hindsight can we see they weren't such a big deal. Some of them we even laugh about years later.

A mother in our congregation told me such a story. When her daughter was twelve, a friend spent the night. The next morning, the woman's fourteen-year-old son came running in and told her, "Mom, you know what

Sis and her friend did while I was sleeping? They shaved my armpits!" Given everything that goes on physically and emotionally with the onset of puberty, that was probably at least a medium-sized stone, so the woman went to her daughter and said, "What on earth were you thinking, shaving your brother's armpits? You are in such big trouble!"

"Mom," said the daughter, "I didn't do that!"

"I know you did," said the mother, but no amount of talking would get the daughter to admit to the prank, despite the evidence of her brother's shaved armpits. So she was grounded.

Ten years later, the son came to his mother. "I have something to confess, Mom. That night, I shaved my own armpits to get Sis in trouble."

Big stone? Small stone? I would guess only that family knows for sure.

Another woman in our congregation told me she had a running battle with her parents about toilet paper! Should it be fed "over the top" or "from below"? The battle had started when she was growing up, but had continued to this day. The woman told me, "Adam, when my mom comes to visit my house, she still changes out all my toilet paper rolls before she leaves!" How serious is this? For some, this would be a small pebble, for others a huge irritant.

Families have plenty of stones, big and small, that they give to and take from each other. It seems almost built into the system. We can hold on to those stones, letting the irritations pile up until our backpacks are full, but if we do, it's tough to maintain any relationship at all with our families. We've got to learn to say, "This may irritate me, but I'm going to let it go."

Let's return to the RAP acronym. Yes, when dropped on us repeatedly by family members, small pebbles can be especially irritating. But if we *remember* our own shortcomings, *assume* the best, and *pray* for God's blessings for the other, we can usually get past the small things—even if they were done by your mom or dad or kid brother or big sister.

If you're an adult and your parents still give you un-
solicited advice, or if your kids have hurt you in some
way, you may try a prayer like this: "God, please bless
my daughter (mother, son, father). I'm assuming she
doesn't really mean what she said and that she doesn't
know it hurts. But I pray you would bless her and help
her to become the woman you want her to be. Make
me a blessing to her. Help me to let go of my frustration
or disappointment or hurt."

## THE BIGGER STONES

Then there are the more serious, medium-sized
stones from family members that include hurtful words,
disrespect, disappointments, and slights that you just
can't shake off. Maybe you were ignored or made to feel
you weren't as important as your sibling. Jacob loaded
up his kids' backpacks with medium-sized stones in just
that way. He provided enough stones to build a wall be-

tween Joseph and his brothers, and that kind of thing happens often in families. In many cases, when others ask for forgiveness, the stones can be let go with relative ease, but when there is no repentance, it becomes harder. Sometimes family members don't think they did anything wrong, or they're convinced they were right no matter what you say. Whatever the case, we pile those stones between us, and the emotional barrier becomes a wall.

There are two ways to break down that wall. One way is for the other family members to understand what they've done and how it affects you. That will sometimes happen after you've talked to them, if you're careful to share your feelings in a way that won't raise their defenses. It may be helpful to go to see a counselor together who can act as an intermediary. After hearing your side of things, the other person may say, "I'm sorry. I didn't realize it affected you that way. I really do love you, and I want to change." Or, they still may be unable to understand.

If the parent, sibling, or child won't sit down with you or meet with a counselor, you'll still need to figure out how to handle the pain and anger. In such cases, you can try the second way to break down the wall: tear it down yourself. You might say, "These stones are not worth the cost of having no relationship with my dad," or, "These rocks are ruining my relationship with my child. I've got to let them go." Then you learn to forgive.

If you've been trying the RAP process but it doesn't seem to be working, you may want to add an S: *seek* to understand. With this additional step, you do your best to understand what has shaped the other person and made them what they are.

Years ago, a group of siblings shared with me how their father had treated them when they were growing up. He never knew how to say he loved them. He wasn't kind or compassionate. He was a hard man, and they carried a lot of pain from their childhood. Then one day, the children found out that when their father was a little boy, his parents had regularly locked him in a closet when he did something wrong. He would be in there with no light, sometimes for hours at a time.

We learn how to parent from our parents, and most of us try not to repeat the negative experiences our parents inflicted on us as children. We want to be the parents our parents were not. In the case of that father, he had vowed not to lock his children in a closet the way his parents had done to him, and he succeeded. He just never took the next step and learned to be tender.

When his children finally understood what had happened, it didn't make everything okay. It did, however, bring them to the point where they could honestly say, "We understand that our father did the best he could."

## THE REALLY BIG STONES

In talking with my congregation about forgiveness and families, I also heard about some really big stones. There were people who had been abandoned by their parents.

There were others whose parents beat them regularly, leaving bruises, welts, and bloody wounds. There were children who, like modern-day Prodigals, took and took from their parents, wasting the family's money or using it to abuse drugs and alcohol. Even as their parents tried to help, the children blamed them and called them names. In one case, parents reported that their children stole from them, leaving their hearts broken and their checkbooks empty, and then refused to talk with them again.

In all, the congregation sent me twenty single-spaced pages of comments about the boulders they carried from relationships with parents or children. This comment was typical of those I received on the subject:

> I was abused and abandoned by both parents growing up. It has totally affected me in my adult life. I have carried this abuse around as shame, and let me tell you, it's like carrying a thousand backpacks on your soul. It ate me up inside for years. I felt like I was worthless, that I didn't really matter. I couldn't be truly intimate with my husband because I had *huge* walls up. I was also full of rage.

The writer went on to describe how she was finally able to let it go. In her case, as in the case of so many in our congregation, the answer was forgiveness.

This wasn't the kind of thing where you say, "Oh, good. I read a book on forgiveness. I'm going to let it go now. I'll just pray about it and it'll all be gone." It doesn't work that way. We chip away slowly at these giant stones and pray that God will help us let go of the pain. But there are certain things we can do to help expedite the process. That's what I heard over and over again from the people who wrote to me. These were not academic solutions. They were the real experiences of real people, sharing about what helped them let go of the stones in their lives.

Many had found help from therapy. They met and worked with counselors who assisted them in analyzing and understanding what had happened, and helped them seek out ways of coping and dealing with the results. There were others who had shared their secret pain with close friends, perhaps with a small group in their church. Their friends helped carry the heavy stones, until finally the wounded ones could let go.

For many, confronting the individual who wounded them was key to their healing and letting go. One person who had been abandoned as a child wrote a letter describing all the things she remembered from her childhood and how she didn't want to be captive to those things anymore. In order to let them go, she had to get them out and on paper. She had to be able to say, "This happened and we have to acknowledge it." She told me, "It was so hard writing every sentence. It was so painful. I had never actually formed those words before. But when I was finished and I sent the letter, it was like a boil had been lanced. I felt like there was the beginning of healing because I finally acknowledged and confronted this."

Many found healing through prayer. One woman said, "Every single day, I would say the Lord's Prayer. I would get to that point where it says, 'Forgive us our trespasses as we forgive those who trespass against us,' and each day, I felt that the stone was being chipped away. I wanted that to happen in my life. I wanted to be that person. And I felt that God began to heal me."

Another woman said that when she was in college, she went to receive the Eucharist every single day at the Episcopal campus ministry. She said there was something about the bread and wine—that just tasting it made her feel the Holy Spirit working to change her and help her and deliver her.

Many people have asked how a person can work through the process of forgiveness with someone who is dead. One man in our church told this story:

I had a dad who was abusive when I was growing up. Then, in the last few years of his life, he actually had to come and live with me because he was physically in need of help. It was a real struggle taking care of a father who had abused me as a child. Right at the end, he took my hand in the hospital. He came as close as he's ever come to saying he loved me, and he thanked me for what I had done in caring for him. And then he died. We never really had a chance to work things out. So, a year after he died, I took a lawn chair, a bottle of wine, and a sandwich to my father's grave. I sat down and talked it all out with him. I told him all the things that had been hurtful to me and told him I forgave him. And I asked him to forgive me for the things I'd done that had been hurtful to him.

Just because the man's father was gone didn't mean they couldn't have that conversation. If we believe that people live on after death, then perhaps God invited the man's father to listen to that graveside conversation. And if his father was not listening, God was.

Finally, many people told me they found healing by looking for ways to bring something good from their pain, asking God to let them help others with similar suffering, so that that their pain might have meaning. A number of these people got to the point where they could thank God—not for the pain, but for the opportunity to use it for good. One young man who had been abused by a babysitter when he was young said it wasn't until he began to help other victims of abuse that he experienced the last bit of his healing.

## JOSEPH'S STORY: PART TWO

It is probable that Joseph held on to the pain of what his brothers had done to him for quite a while. We know that, once in Egypt, he became the slave of a man named Potiphar. Potiphar's wife tried to seduce Joseph, and when he refused, she falsely accused him of attempted rape. He was wrongly convicted and thrown into prison. His life seemed to go from bad to worse. But he refused to turn his back on God. I imagine him praying something like, "God, please do something with these terrible circumstances. I can't change what's happened in the past, but I pray that you might reshape the future."

We don't know how long Joseph was enslaved or in prison, but somehow during those years something happened to him. The bad things he had gone through began to shape his character in a positive way. He seemed to have been able to give his pain over to God. His soul had deepened, his dependence on God had strengthened, and his suffering had changed him from a narcissistic boy into a man of compassion and integrity.

Then one day, Joseph's ability to interpret dreams— the skill that had gotten him into so much trouble as a boy—became known in prison and ultimately to Pharaoh. So when Pharaoh began having terrible dreams that no one could interpret, he called Joseph, who said the dreams foretold a famine. Thereafter, in a dramatic reversal of fortunes, Joseph became the trusted advisor to Pharaoh and eventually the chief governor of Egypt. He was charged with leading Egypt's efforts to prepare for the famine and to oversee food distribution when famine came.

The famine also struck the land of Canaan, where Joseph's brothers had long since forgotten him but where his father still grieved. The sons were forced to go to Egypt to buy grain. There, as they stood before the chief governor, they discovered to their great surprise and dismay that the man who would determine whether they would receive grain and survive the famine was none other than the younger brother they had sold into slavery.

Joseph's life had come full circle. Yet, had his brothers not sold him into slavery and Potiphar's wife not accused him falsely, he would not have been in this position to save his family. Joseph was able to look back and see God's hand working through all the things that had happened. He had relinquished control to God, trusting that God would chip away at the pain of the past and produce something beautiful, and it had come to pass.

As the Apostle Paul wrote many years later, "In all things God works for the good of those who love him, who have been called according to his purpose." As we now know, the climactic example of God's working for good was Jesus' death on the cross. So much more terrible than the troubles of Joseph, this incident was used by God for the redemption of the world. The cross thus became the central symbol of the Christian faith, and through it, the world was changed. The cross teaches us that God can take the pain and suffering of our past, when we put them into his hands, and produce something beautiful. That is why some have defined forgiveness as "giving up the hope of a different past." I would add to this that it's taking on the hope of a joyful future. Forgiveness is believing that the future can be better than the past. The past can't be changed, but God can do something redemptive with it.

Joseph's story ended with his brothers bowing down before him, just as he had dreamed when he was a boy. When he revealed himself to them—the betrayed little brother now Pharaoh's right-hand man—they were convinced that Joseph would kill them. If the tables had been turned, they certainly would have done something like that to him. But, on the contrary, it is just at that moment in the Bible that we come to the book's first use of the word forgive. Joseph's brothers asked for forgiveness, and Joseph extended it. His words to them were profound, as captured in Genesis 50:20: "'Even though you intended to do harm to me, God intended it for good, in order to preserve a numerous people, as he is doing today. So have no fear; I myself will provide for you and your little ones.' In this way he reassured them, speaking kindly to them."

That day, Joseph's brothers asked for forgiveness, and Joseph chose to forgive. That day, Joseph and his brothers wept, and were reconciled to one another in a profound picture of grace and healing.

In like manner, one woman in our congregation wrote,

> You can choose to harm everyone because you were hurt, or you can choose to harm no one because you were hurt. Either way, it's a choice. It's so easy to fall into the trap of victimhood and choose the former, but thankfully God gives us a divine capacity for love and forgiveness. And when we use that gift, it fills our lives with so much joy

that it's impossible to be resentful to those who do not
have that same joy in their lives.

The woman went on to quote the chorus of an old
Shaker hymn:

> No storm can shake my inmost calm
> While to that rock I'm clinging.
> Since love is Lord of heaven and earth,
> How can I keep from singing?

The rock the singer clings to is, of course, not one of
the rocks we've been talking about. The Bible says that
Jesus is the stone the builders rejected, the stone that
became the cornerstone. She clings to Jesus.

## OUR STONES

Jesus trained to be a carpenter under his earthly father, Joseph, and probably practiced the trade until he

was twenty-nine. Some years ago, when I was in Israel, I had a chance to visit the excavated ruins of the once-bustling town of Tzippori or Sepphoris, which was likely the place where Joseph and Jesus practiced their trade. There, I saw houses from the first century and often wondered, "Did Jesus and Joseph help build this house?"

I noticed something, though. The houses in that town were not built of wood, but of stone. Jesus was a stonemason, shaping stone and bringing something good from it. He can do the same thing with our stones—taking them, working away at them, and doing something good with something bad. He does this little by little, day by day, whenever we place our stones in his hands.

If you are carrying a stone, big or small, it's time to let it go. I invite you to take the first step and bring it to God. Lay it in his hands, place it on his altar, and say, "God, please take these things from the past. Do something good with them and help me let them go." Many people I've spoken with have told me that one particular prayer helped them a great deal as they worked through painful situations. It's a prayer most of us are familiar with. Our friends in Alcoholics Anonymous have adopted it. It was written in 1934 by the great protestant theologian Reinhold Niebuhr, and it is called the Serenity Prayer:

> God, grant me the serenity to accept the things I cannot change, the courage to change the things I can, and the wisdom to know the difference. Living one day at a time, enjoying one moment at a time, accepting hardships as the pathway to peace, taking as he did this sinful world as it is, not as I would have it, trusting that he will make all things right if I surrender to his will so that I may be reasonably happy in this life and supremely happy with him forever and ever in the next.

## THINKING IT THROUGH

• Compare the version of Joseph's story presented in this chapter with versions you may remember from your childhood or from the musical *Joseph and the Amazing Technicolor Dreamcoat*. What differences in tone and feeling do you notice? What can you learn from each version?

• Do you know families in which one child appeared to be favored over the others? To the extent that you feel comfortable, describe the situation. What effects did it have on the other children? On the favored child?

• Many of the stones we exchange in families have to do with others' "hot buttons," which seem to persist into adulthood. What are some examples from your family? What have you done or what could you do to alleviate some of those hot buttons?

• As you read the story of the man confronting his dead father, how did you feel? Is this something you would do? Why or why not?

• What stones are you carrying in your backpack? What would it take for you to let go of them?

# IN GOD'S IMAGE

*God created humankind in his image,*
*in the image of God he created them;*
*male and female he created them.*

*Genesis 1:27*

Forgiveness is powerful.

The Bible begins with the story of creation. The "image of God" referred to in the story—*imago Dei* in Latin—has nothing to do with our physical appearance, and everything to do with other ways in which we were created to reflect the character of God. We were created with the capacity to love, to reason, to create, to show compassion, to give, to sacrifice, and, yes, to forgive.

Tragically the *imago Dei* in us is often obscured. Adam and Eve chose to eat the forbidden fruit and paradise was lost. Cain became jealous of his brother Abel and bashed Abel's brains in. Lamech wasn't satisfied with one wife; he needed two, so he sought retribution and killed a man who had wounded him. And all this happens in just the first five chapters of the Bible! By the events in chapter 6, God's image in the world was so obscured that God grieved about ever creating human beings.

We refer to the cause and the results of this distortion of God's image by using the same word, *sin*—straying from God's way. As we learned previously, sin signifies both the condition of our hearts, and the acts we commit because of that condition. It is sin that often leads us to say and do things for which we need forgiveness. And it is sin that sometimes keeps us from seeking or extending forgiveness. But when we do ask for or extend forgiveness, we live into the *imago Dei*. It is for this reason that I think forgiveness, when extended, is not only powerful but beautiful.

Several years ago, Victoria Ruvolo of New York was selected as that year's "Most Inspiring Person" by *Beliefnet,* an online faith community. A group of teenagers had used a stolen credit card to go shopping and had bought, among other things, a frozen turkey. As they were driving, one of teenagers, a young man named Ryan, decided to throw the turkey out the car window into oncoming traffic. The turkey smashed through Ruvolo's windshield, crushing her face. She survived the accident but required ten hours of reconstructive surgery and a tracheotomy tube. That fall, Victoria attended Ryan's sentencing. To everyone's surprise, she asked the judge to be lenient toward the young man, noting, "Each day I thank God simply because I'm alive. I sincerely hope you have also learned from this awful experience, Ryan. There is no room in my life for vengeance." Ryan wept and expressed remorse for his action, and was sentenced to six months in prison rather than the maximum twenty-five years. That day Victoria went on to tell Ryan, "I truly hope that by demonstrating compassion and leniency I have encouraged you to seek an honorable life. If my generosity will help you mature into a responsible, honest man whose graciousness is a source of pride to your loved ones and your community, then I will be truly gratified, and my suffering will not have been in vain. . . . Ryan, prove me right" (Leah Ingram, "Compassionate victim," www .beliefnet.com [December 2005]).

Victoria Ruvolo's story demonstrates redemption, mercy, and grace. It resonates with us at a deep level, because in it we see the image of God.

The world saw that same image when Nelson Mandela, after being imprisoned by South Africa's apartheid government for twenty-seven years, called upon black South Africans to demonstrate love instead of hate, and modeled this mercy in his own life in powerful ways.

His call for mercy helped prevent the bloody violence many had anticipated with the fall of apartheid. The world saw the *imago Dei* in this act, not only of Mandela but of black South Africans.

Twice the Apostle Paul describes Jesus as the "image of God" (2 Corinthians 4:4 and Colossians 1:15). Jesus came to restore humanity—to recover and heal the image of God in us. In his life, death, and resurrection, Jesus not only offers forgiveness and redemption but also shows us the *imago Dei* that we were meant to exhibit and that, through the ongoing work of the Holy Spirit in us, we might yet one day exhibit.

Jesus constantly spoke of forgiveness. But on the cross he demonstrated it when he prayed, "Father, forgive them; for they do not know what they are doing" (Luke 23:34). I believe there may have been a man named Stephen in the crowd that day who heard Jesus utter the prayer. Stephen was not one of the apostles but was a follower of Jesus. We can imagine that Jesus' example of mercy deeply moved Stephen, and he would never forget it. Jesus' words painted a picture of the *imago Dei* that may have shaped how Stephen would live the rest of his life.

We know, following the resurrection of Christ, that Stephen was chosen by the apostles to serve the fledgling church, ministering to those in need while sharing the gospel with all who would listen, and that he was "full of grace and power" (Acts 6:8). Stephen's life and ministry were so compelling that some who opposed the Christian faith began to speak ill of him. They stirred up others against him, making false accusations that Stephen had blasphemed against God. He was arrested and accused before the same ruling council that had sentenced Jesus to death and for his blasphemy was sentenced to death by stoning. Stephen's death is described in Acts:

> They dragged him out of the city and began to stone him; and the witnesses laid their coats at the feet of a young man named Saul. While they were stoning Stephen, he

prayed, "Lord Jesus, receive my spirit." Then he knelt down and cried out in a loud voice, "Lord, do not hold this sin against them." When he had said this, he died. And Saul approved of their killing him. (Acts 7:58–8:1)

Saul stood watching as Stephen, like the righteous Abel, was put to death. Once more we see the distortion of God's image in this act of cruelty portraying itself as religious devotion. Saul would be haunted by what he heard and saw that day. He would never forget the way Stephen knelt and prayed as he was being stoned, "Lord, do not hold this sin against them." In this remarkable act of mercy, the seeds were sown that would lead to Saul's own conversion to Christ, after which he would be known as Paul the Apostle. Mercy has the power to change even the hardest of hearts.

In 1994, Americans Reginald and Margaret Green were vacationing with their children in the southern Italian region of Calabria. As they were driving down the highway, robbers approached their car, thinking it belonged to a local jeweler. They shot into the car multiple times, striking seven-year-old Nicholas, who was sitting in the backseat. Nicholas was taken to the hospital and later died. Italians in the area were stricken with grief and shame for the death of this little boy.

What made the Greens' story most remarkable was the fact that, before their son was taken off life support, they donated his organs and saved the lives of seven Italians. Their gift, an expression of mercy in the face of a horrible crime, deeply moved the Italian people. It was a profoundly beautiful picture of the *imago Dei* we were meant to embody. Both the president and the prime minister of Italy, upon hearing of the Greens' gift, called personally upon the family. The nation was so moved by the story that organ donations increased fourfold in response. Thousands of lives were saved.

I'll share with you one final story, not so much to illustrate the concept of forgiveness as to remind you of its urgency. Several years ago, a member of my congregation died suddenly, and over the next few days, as family and friends came to pay their respects, it became obvious to me that a number of them longed for reconciliation. Some wanted to forgive the man who had died; others wanted his forgiveness. All of them had assumed there would be time to reconcile, and they were wrong. During those days and in the years after, they struggled with feelings of regret. Some of them still may be struggling.

If there's someone in your life you long to forgive, or whose forgiveness you seek, don't wait. Go to that person. Begin the conversation. You may not get everything you seek, but you will know you tried, and the rest you can leave in God's hands.

Shakespeare wrote of mercy, "It is an attribute of God himself" and "it blesseth him that gives and him that takes." We need it, and to be fully human we must also freely extend it. After all, as Paul Tillich wrote, "forgiveness is an answer, the divine answer, to the question implied in our existence."

That, finally, is the power of the gospel message.

God, whose love we have spurned and whose ways we have rejected, sends his son to suffer and die to procure and proclaim our forgiveness. We look at the cross and hear Jesus crying out, "Father, forgive them!" This act of mercy, when finally apprehended, has the power to set us free from guilt, to turn us away from our sin and toward the God whose mercy we've been offered. This picture of a God who forgives, who offers mercy, which by its definition is undeserved, has moved Western civilization away from an ideal of retribution to an ideal of redemption and forgiveness.

When we choose to show mercy, the image of God is seen in us. Our willingness to forgive has the power not only to change us, freeing us from bitterness and resentment but to change those who receive mercy from us, just as we are changed when finally we see and comprehend the vast and wonderful mercy of God.

*Lord, have mercy upon me. Forgive me for the ways I have given offense to you, whether in thought, word, or deed, or by things I have done or left undone. Even as I ask for your mercy, help me be merciful to those who wrong me. Help me let go of the need for retribution and to extend grace freely to others. Finally, Lord, convict me of the ways I've wounded others, and help me seek reconciliation with them—not tomorrow or next week, but today, so that they, and I, may be free. Lord, have mercy upon me. In Jesus' name. Amen*

# ACKNOWLEDGMENTS

This book would not be possible without the people of the United Methodist Church of the Resurrection. Each year I survey the congregation asking about their needs, questions, and concerns that might be addressed in a sermon series. Forgiveness regularly comes up as a concern. This book is based on a sermon series I preached in response to that issue, focused on the questions and concerns they raised.

In addition, each week as I was preparing the sermons I invited members of the church to collaborate with me, and in response they shared their stories illustrating the various dimensions of forgiveness. I'm also grateful to the worship planning team and our pastors at Resurrection, who helped shape the themes and ideas as I outlined the sermons.

Finally, special thanks to Rob Simbeck and Ron Kidd. Rob's work in transforming my sermon manuscripts into chapters for this book has been invaluable, and Ron's editorial revisions and suggestions have made this a much better book than it would have been without him.

# WHY?

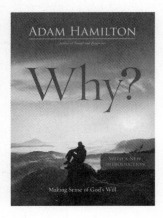

When the ground shakes, and a poor nation's economy is destroyed; when the waters rise, washing away a community's hopes and dreams; when a child suffers neglect and abuse; when violence tears apart nations: Where is God? In *Why? Making Sense of God's Will*, best-selling author Adam Hamilton brings fresh insight to the age-old question of how to understand the will of God. Rejecting simplistic answers and unexamined assumptions, Hamilton addresses how we can comprehend God's plan for the world and ourselves.

Read *Why?* on your own or, for a more in-depth study, enjoy it with a small group.

**ISBN 978-1-5018-5828-4**

"I recommend this book to anyone who longs to leave behind simplistic answers and discover a God who invites them into a collaborative process of bringing redemption, love, and hope to a world in desperate need."

—**Lynne Hybels**, author of *Nice Girls Don't Change the World*

Available wherever fine books are sold.

For more information about Adam Hamilton, visit www.AdamHamilton.org

# ENOUGH

Money has great power in our lives. Used wisely, it is one key to accomplishing our goals, providing for our needs, and fulfilling our life purpose. However, ignoring the wisdom of the past when it comes to managing and spending our money can lead to greater stress and anxiety. *Enough* is an invitation to rediscover the Bible's wisdom when it comes to prudent financial practices. In its pages are found the keys to experiencing contentment, overcoming fear, and discovering joy through simplicity and generosity.

Read *Enough* on your own or, for a more in-depth study, enjoy it with a small group.

**ISBN 978-1-5018-5788-1**

"We Americans love our stuff. We're living in a fast-paced, me-first, instant-gratification world, and it's finally catching up to us. Debt is out of control, homes are in foreclosure ... even banks are going out of business. What the world needs today is the message of contentment and simplicity, and that's exactly what Pastor Adam Hamilton delivers in *Enough*."

—**Dave Ramsey**, *New York Times* Best-Selling Author and Nationally Syndicated Radio Talk Show Host

Available wherever fine books are sold.

For more information about Adam Hamilton, visit www.AdamHamilton.org

# THE JOURNEY

Journey with Adam Hamilton as he travels from Nazareth to Bethlehem in this fascinating look at the birth of Jesus Christ. As he did with Jesus' crucifixion in *24 Hours That Changed the World,* Hamilton once again approaches a world-changing event with thoughtfulness. Using historical information, archaeological data, and a personal look at some of the stories surrounding the birth, the most amazing moment in history will become more real and heartfelt as you walk along this road.

Read *The Journey* on your own or, for a more in-depth study, enjoy it with a small group.

**ISBN 978-1-5018-2879-9**
**ISBN 978-1-5018-3604-6 Large Print**

Available wherever fine books are sold.
For more information about Adam Hamilton, visit www.AdamHamilton.org

# CONTINUE THE JOURNEY

Go deeper on your Christmas journey with *A Season of Reflection*. With Scripture, stories, and prayer, this collection of 28 daily readings brings the well-known story into your daily spiritual life.

**ISBN 978-1-4267-1426-9**

Join Adam Hamilton as he travels the roads to Bethlehem in this video journey. In five video segments, Adam explores Bethlehem, the routes the Holy Family traveled, the traditional site of the stable in Bethlehem, the ruins of Herodium, and more.

**ISBN 978-1-4267-1999-8**

*Study resources for children, youth, and adults and
an app for families are also available.*
**Learn more at JourneyThisChristmas.com**

Available wherever fine books are sold.
For more information about Adam Hamilton, visit www.AdamHamilton.org

# THE WAY

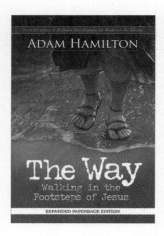

Travel to the Holy Land in this third volume of Adam Hamilton's Bible study trilogy on the life of Jesus. Once again, Hamilton approaches his subject matter with thoughtfulness and wisdom as he did with Jesus' crucifixion in *24 Hours That Changed the World* and with Jesus' birth in *The Journey*. Using historical background, archaeological findings, and stories of the faith, Hamilton retraces the footsteps of Jesus from his baptism to the temptations to the heart of his ministry, including the people he loved, the enemies he made, the parables he taught, and the roads that he traveled.

Read *The Way* on your own or, for a more in-depth study, enjoy it with a small group.

**ISBN 978-1-5018-2878-2**
**ISBN 978-1-5018-3606-0 Large print**

# CONTINUE THE WAY

This companion volume to *The Way* functions beautifully on its own or as part of the churchwide experience. Adam Hamilton offers daily devotions that enable us to pause, meditate, and emerge changed forever. Ideal for use during Lent, the reflections include Scripture, stories from Hamilton's own ministry, and prayers.

**ISBN 978-1-4267-5252-0**

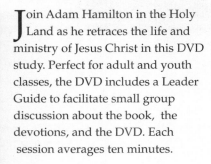

Join Adam Hamilton in the Holy Land as he retraces the life and ministry of Jesus Christ in this DVD study. Perfect for adult and youth classes, the DVD includes a Leader Guide to facilitate small group discussion about the book, the devotions, and the DVD. Each session averages ten minutes.

**ISBN 978-1-4267-5253-7**

*Study resources for children, youth, and adults are also available.*

Available wherever fine books are sold.

For more information about Adam Hamilton, visit www.AdamHamilton.org

# 24 HOURS THAT CHANGED THE WORLD

Walk with Jesus on his final day. Sit beside him at the Last Supper. Pray with him in Gethsemane. Follow him to the cross. Desert him. Deny him. Experience the Resurrection.

No single event in human history has received more attention than the suffering and crucifixion of Jesus of Nazareth. In this heartbreaking, inspiring book, Adam Hamilton guides us, step by step, through the last 24 hours of Jesus' life.

Read *24 Hours That Changed the World* on your own or, for a more in-depth study, enjoy it with a small group.

**ISBN 978-0-687-46555-2**
**ISBN 978-1-5018-3606-0 Large print**

"Adam Hamilton combines biblical story, historical detail, theological analysis, and spiritual insight, and pastoral warmth to retell the narrative of Jesus' last and greatest hours."
—**Leith Anderson,** author of *The Jesus Revolution*

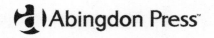

Available wherever fine books are sold.
For more information about Adam Hamilton, visit www.AdamHamilton.org